Victoria Worsley

Victoria Worsley MA, FG(UK) was an actor, movement director and theatre-maker for twenty years. She discovered the Feldenkrais Method at the age of seventeen whilst studying movement for performance with Monika Pagneux (a colleague of Dr Feldenkrais). She has explored and used the Method ever since, especially following a debilitating knee injury in 1996.

She qualified as a professional Feldenkrais practitioner in Lewes in 2007 and now has a busy general practice in North London where she sees people from all walks of life, aged from a few months old to later stages of life. They come to regain or improve skills for all kinds of performance, sport, martial arts or yoga; to reduce chronic pain; recover from injury; work with a neurological condition or just have a better quality of life.

Victoria has taught Feldenkrais in drama schools since 2008, as well as at the Actors Centre in London, and for other performance companies and organisations. She also coaches actors on an individual basis. Victoria is married with a teenage daughter, she likes to run (barefoot where possible), and is training for her black belt in traditional Okinawan Goju Ryu Karate.

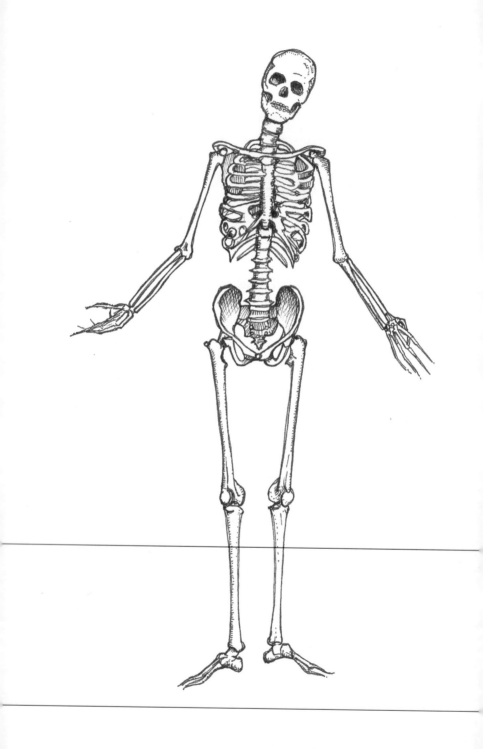

FELDENKRAIS
for ACTORS
How to Do Less and Discover More

Victoria Worsley

Illustrated by James Humphries

NICK HERN BOOKS
London
www.nickhernbooks.co.uk

A Nick Hern Book

Feldenkrais for Actors
first published in Great Britain in 2016
by Nick Hern Books Limited,
The Glasshouse, 49a Goldhawk Road, London W12 8QP

Reprinted 2018

Cover photograph © Judy Bould
Designed and typeset by Nick Hern Books
Printed and bound in Great Britain by
Ashford Colour Press, Gosport, Hampshire

A CIP catalogue record for this book is available
from the British Library

ISBN 978 1 84842 417 3

Contents

Foreword *by John Wright*

It's a truism to say that the way we feel affects the things we do, but the fact is inescapable. I see it dampen possibilities in every rehearsal and in every workshop, as people struggle with what they want to do, and what they think they can't. Old habits, old movement patterns – some as old as childhood – are imprinted on our minds and re-released in the way we move. The Feldenkrais Method is unique in my experience in interceding between the glib personal assumptions we make about ourselves, and our actual potential.

Before I started doing Feldenkrais, I used to think that to make any progress in movement work, it had to hurt. 'No pain – no gain' was the prevailing culture in my previous training, but Feldenkrais continually teaches me that the reverse is true: if you feel the pain, there'll be no gain. It's the essential lesson of less doing more, where the journey is more important than the arrival, and where the desire to achieve is the greatest obstacle to doing anything. In my experience, this reckless economy starts with the rediscovery of simple functional movement, such as the journey from lying to standing, or from walking to running, and running to jumping.

But the implications of the work go way beyond this. I feel less fatigue when I've done some Feldenkrais, and big new challenges fall into more comfortable proportions. I think more clearly. I'm more aware, more present; yet at the same time, more objective. I feel as if my ego has been switched off, and I find it easier to take on new ideas, to do something different – something else.

I haven't found any other movement study that opens up such a rich and continuing area of enquiry. It's as if I'm taken back to the place that nature intended me to be, rather than keeping me at the place where life has left me. And all this through the gentle art of teaching yourself not to try.

John Wright is a theatre-maker, director and teacher, and co-founder of Trestle Theatre Company and Told by an Idiot. His books include Why Is That So Funny? A Practical Exploration of Physical Comedy.

Introduction

Movement is Life

I was looking on a forum where actors left comments about their experience of drama school, and in the discussions of movement lessons I found everything from 'The Most Useful Thing I Ever Did' to the marvellous title of 'Wanky Movement'. I am sure neither of these actors is alone in their opinions. However, instead of asking why would you want to study movement as an actor throughout your career, I would like to turn it around and ask: why on earth *wouldn't* you? If someone said to you that there is something which is absolutely integral to people's characteristics of behaviour, which governs how they do anything, reveals who they are, and is so fundamental to life that no one would even be able to stay alive without it – wouldn't you, as an actor or person who works with actors, want to know as much about it as you possibly could? I do find these days that more actors and students have an expectation that they will study movement, but it's still worth having a look at the question to understand why an approach like Feldenkrais is useful. Forgive me if you need no convincing.

Moshe Feldenkrais always stressed that there is no life without movement. Everything you do to stay alive or continue the species involves movement: breathing, seeing, getting food or drink, chewing, swallowing, defecating, urinating, having sex, giving birth, communicating, escaping danger, fighting. No movement: no life.

Then think about the different skills and strengths people develop in their lives and in the jobs they do, such as building, digging, lifting, typing, drawing, sculpting, cleaning, cooking, sewing, painting, singing, playing an instrument, playing a sport, dancing in many varied ways, driving, skating, learning a fighting style and so on. Wouldn't it be surprising if what you did a lot of in your life *didn't* shape you? And what about all those descriptions of people that imply a quality of movement: spineless, slippery, solid, flaky, 'stiff upper lip', strong, weak, withdrawn, outgoing, impetuous, tenacious? Can you laugh, cry, smile, get angry without involving movement? Movement is the stuff of life. Literally. So why on earth wouldn't you study it in a myriad of ways to be an actor? Wouldn't it, in fact, be completely weird *not* to do so?

It is worth making those observations even if they turn out to be obvious to some, because when you consider *how* you might learn something about how movement shapes people (how they behave, how they communicate, the quality they bring to any simple task or interaction), you realise you need a very particular kind of process.

Any study of movement that is going to help you learn these kinds of things is unlikely to be about press-ups, weights, stretching and doing the splits. Those things can be fun and help you feel good and might be part of what's needed for a specific role or a requirement for a style of theatre (some of those things might even have a contribution to health or fitness), but they are not going to help you learn much about different ways and qualities of behaving, being or doing. Moreover, exploring behaving, being and doing is notoriously tricky and can be very challenging because any process devoted to it is also bound to reveal something about who and how you are: your edges and limitations as a person. And then any such process may feel a little strange and unusual because the territory, as well as the means, is likely to be unfamiliar. Mechanical exercise, which we tend to be more used to, just doesn't cut it here. It can't do the job of delving into human behaviour in all its rich variety and subtlety.

You may find a process that does address the job liberating, exciting and unbelievably interesting. Or you may want to call it 'wanky movement'. If the latter is true, there are other ways in. However, in the end you will come up against patterns and habits of movement because they are fundamental to patterns and habits of human behaviour, and exploring human behaviour is what an actor does. So at some point you will probably just have to get over yourself and learn how to work with movement in some way if you want to develop further. It's true that everyone has limitations to who and how they can be, but many also accept unnecessary limitations to their skill, artistry and casting by hiding behind 'It's not me', whether they are the student who can't deal with 'wanky movement' or the seasoned actor simply stuck in a comfortable (or uncomfortable) rut.

The Feldenkrais Method uses movement in a great variety of structured ways to enable you to explore how you personally respond or do things; to open up new avenues and expand your possibilities. It is not a complete study of acting all on its own, of course, and there are other movement methods that complement it and take some aspects further. However, as its focus is on the fundamentals of human functioning and developing potential, and as it enables people to experience what they do clearly and to travel beyond their habits in ways they may not have been able to envisage otherwise, it is a very valuable Method for actors. It's like giving them a box of toys to play with that they didn't know they had. In fact, there are very many more ways that the Method works for actors, but I will unpack them as we progress.

Frank Wildman – dancer, performer and Feldenkrais trainer who studied with Moshe Feldenkrais and was in one of his legendary workshops with Peter Brook's Company (CIRT) – told me that while Feldenkrais worked with many kinds of people from all walks of life (as all Feldenkrais teachers do), he thought his work could be most fully embodied in an actor because they needed to address the use of themselves in every way.

What This Book Is – and Is Not

This book is addressed to students of acting and to actors, directors, makers and teachers of anything to do with performance. No book could claim to be the *only* book on Feldenkrais for actors. This one is just my book. Another practitioner will no doubt have other things to say and other ways to say it. It represents my study and my experience of Feldenkrais since I discovered it while training as an actor with Philippe Gaulier and Monika Pagneux twenty-nine years ago. The Method has been part of my life since then through twenty years as an actor, theatre-maker and occasional movement director, and another nine as a professional Feldenkrais practitioner. I now teach in drama schools and other professional acting organisations and offer one-to-one coaching for actors. I also work with singers, dancers, musicians, martial artists, runners and people from many other walks of life.

It is not an academic book, although I hope the academics will find enough to enjoy. It is intended more for practitioners of theatre and film, and students heading into the business. However, it is also not a complete 'how-to' manual. If you find you do want to really learn the Feldenkrais Method, look for a teacher (see the Appendix). I have included lessons and games as practical examples to give you a taste, but these are only a very few of the several thousands of lessons available.

Please do not think that this book will enable you to teach the Feldenkrais Method as such either. It is not possible to read a book or do one or two workshops and 'know' the Method. It takes four years' study to become even the most basic of professional practitioners, and then you have your learner plates on for several years until you have spent thousands of hours gaining experience. The process itself is humbling for many of us who started as professionals in one line or another thinking we knew something about Feldenkrais, as, in my experience, it is only when you are some way down the line of professional study that you realise just how enormous the possibilities are and how comparatively little you actually know about the work. Of course, even in the first lesson you learn something, and so it is a rewarding journey right from the start. It is not that you have to study and wait for years for any benefit as a student. It may also give you ideas you wish to share, which is legitimate – but the understanding is cumulative and involves a long process of gradually piecing it together and finding ever-deeper layers and connections in order to teach it fully. In fact, you can keep deepening your understanding for the whole of your life as there is nothing more complex than the study of life itself, which is ultimately what this Method turns out to be. Great! It would be boring otherwise, wouldn't it? If you could learn it in a couple of weeks, what would be its worth? Really? I hope this book will give you background, context, ideas and understanding of the kinds of things you could find, develop and explore if you went further.

- Can you become a good actor without this work? Of course. It would be ridiculous to suggest otherwise.

- Can a very experienced actor improve further with this kind of work? Of course. Everyone needs to continue to explore and develop, otherwise they stagnate: at any stage in your career the Feldenkrais Method can offer you a way to delve deeper and improve.

- Will everyone want to learn this way? No. Nothing is for everyone. There are many paths to the top of the mountain.

However, the Feldenkrais Method does encompass a unique and profound understanding of human functioning and of how you are *you* – and the detail of it is like nothing I have come across elsewhere. What I do hope this book will do is go some way to enabling you to understand some of what is very useful about that process for actors, so that you are encouraged to go out and try it for yourself.

Dr Moshe Feldenkrais
© International Feldenkrais Federation Archive

A Little Bit of History

In our work there are elements which are mysterious and elements which are precise. I think we both share the desire, and even the need, to reduce that element of obscurity in theatre practice which depends on unknowables like 'inspiration' and 'genius' to a minimum and to make the craft of our profession as clear as possible.

The very foundation of the work for every actor is their own body – and nothing is more concrete... In Moshe Feldenkrais, I have eventually met someone from a scientific background, who has an all-encompassing mastery of his subject. He has studied the body in movement with a precision that I have never found anything like anywhere else.

For him, the body is a whole. Starting from this concept, he has developed his teaching method in which much of both Eastern and Western systems can be found. Through the workshops that he has led all through his life, in Europe as well as in the United States, he has been able to put together hundreds of exercises of exceptional value.

From a letter by Peter Brook, 1978
(translated from French by Victoria Worsley)

Moshe Feldenkrais

Santa Juan Bautista, Northern California, June 1973. It is very hot. Gathered in a large warehouse in the fields are members of Peter Brook's company of actors who have been travelling through Africa for the last year, improvising on a carpet in villages and towns, seeking to find a totally new form of 'universal' theatre and developing a show based on the myth of *The Conference of the Birds*; members of El Teatro Campesino, a politically based theatre company formed in response to the plight of migrant farmworkers in California; and a few other artists including dancer Frank Wildman, then aged about twenty, now Dr Frank Wildman, a highly experienced Feldenkrais trainer.

This is the first day of an eight-week workshop lead by a sixty-nine-year-old nuclear physicist with a background in engineering and a second-degree black belt in Judo. Dr Moshe Feldenkrais is a man of extraordinary intelligence, with a great breadth of understanding, enormous curiosity and the capacity to transform discoveries in the fields of neuroscience, psychology and human development into practical ways of enabling others to develop their potential through movement. In the first lesson he invites the actors to stand on their hands, bend one knee so one foot can be placed on the wall, lengthen the other leg to the ceiling, push with that foot on the wall and twist the chest until they can take one hand from the floor and put it behind their back. No one can do it except the actor Yoshi Oida.

I don't know how Peter Brook and Moshe Feldenkrais met, and my search to find out has yielded no complete answer so far.[1] In the letter quoted above, it sounds like Brook may have been on a search for someone with the kind of understanding Feldenkrais had, and been introduced to him or stumbled across him somehow. But when and how?

Perhaps it's worth a little detour here to sketch in some of Moshe Feldenkrais's extraordinary story up to that point. He was born into a Hasidic community in a Jewish area of Russia, now Ukraine. Hasidism has a life-affirming tradition of healers and while Feldenkrais was not a religious man, he clearly felt an allegiance with the wisdom of his forebears. The Jews were massacred in that area more than once, first by the Russians and then by the Germans, so, aged fourteen, Feldenkrais set out on foot, without his family, to travel to the British Mandate for Palestine, gathering more and more young people as he went. There he worked hard labouring to help build Tel Aviv as well as studying both at high school and on his own. He had a good grasp of higher mathematics and was employed by the British to help map Palestine, as he was one of the few people there who could do the necessary 'Gaussian Distribution of Errors'. While he was there he also worked out how to fight for his life unarmed against an armed attack,[2] and even wrote a handbook on self-defence for the early Jewish defence force (The Haganah). He left Palestine to study engineering and gain his doctorate at the Sorbonne in Paris, and then moved on to nuclear physics. He was working on a particle accelerator to split the atom in the laboratory of Joliot-Curie when the war broke out.[3]

It was in Paris that Feldenkrais met Jigaro Kano, the founder of Judo.[4] Kano was impressed with his little booklet on self-defence and, seeing in Feldenkrais someone who could help bring his ideas to the West, persuaded him to study Judo. Feldenkrais was among the first Westerners to gain a second-degree black belt, wrote several books on Judo[5] and co-founded the Judo club of France (still in existence today). Indeed, there is much in the Feldenkrais Method that is drawn from his understanding of practising and teaching Judo, and we will see something of the usefulness of martial-arts ideas for actors in this book too. It is also good to keep sight of the notion that, while the Method uses a lot of small, slow movement, it is for the sake of learning and not for the sake of always moving slowly and gently. The Method facilitates all kinds of action, including sports and fighting – indeed, Feldenkrais's interest lay in enabling people to find their 'potency' and live more fully.

Feldenkrais came to the UK fleeing the Nazis' advance, clasping the nuclear secrets and a jar of heavy water from the laboratory, and was recruited by the British Admiralty to help with sonar research.[6] He also trained a British battalion in strangulation techniques – you can still buy his handbook![7] During this period he continued to work with his own old footballing knee injury (torn cruciate ligaments and damaged cartilage for which there was no neat keyhole surgery in those days), and was also working on the ways of learning through movement that led to the development of the Method. In 1949 he wrote his first landmark book on these ideas, *Body and Mature Behaviour*. In 1951 he was asked back to the newly created state of Israel to work for the military and answered the call, but at the same time he also began giving lessons to the President, Ben Gurion, who soon found many opportunities to talk about Feldenkrais and his Method. There is a famous photograph of Ben Gurion standing on his head on the beach – something Feldenkrais had taught him – and Garet Newell told me a saying that puts it well: 'Feldenkrais put Ben Gurion on his head and Ben Gurion put Feldenkrais on his feet.' From this time, Feldenkrais finally devoted himself entirely to the development of this aspect of his work.

To come back now to the question we began with – how and why Feldenkrais and Peter Brook met – the latter had started working in the theatre in 1943, was already Director of Productions at the Royal Opera House by 1947, and went to the Royal Shakespeare Company in 1950, so there was time for him and Feldenkrais to meet each other in the UK professionally, socially or perhaps even through their shared interest in a philosopher called Gurdjieff.[8]

By the time of the Santa Juan Bautista workshop in 1973, Feldenkrais had already worked with Peter Brook's International Centre for Theatre Research (CIRT) on a few occasions since its inception in 1970/1, and would continue to work at its new home at the Bouffes Du Nord in Paris every May for some years.

According to Brook's letter, he was still teaching actors at Bouffes Du Nord in 1978. However, soon after the Santa Juan Bautista workshop, he also began teaching on the first professional training programme in the US. This was in San Francisco in 1975–8. A second followed in Amherst starting in 1980, which was attended by over two hundred students. The trainings ran for nine weeks a year for four years each, but Feldenkrais only completed the first two years of the Amherst training and died after a series of strokes in 1984. His assistants – from among the small group he had already previously trained in Israel – completed the training between them, sowing the seeds for one of the most sophisticated approaches to human development today.

This Method can enable those with cerebral palsy (even tiny children), stroke or other nervous-system disorders, as well as those who just want to recover from injury or get out of chronic pain. It can also benefit musicians, dancers, actors, singers, martial artists and sportspeople of all kinds, or those who simply want to enjoy their daily lives more fully. He was – and in some ways still is – ahead of his time. Some of the better known who have experienced his or his descendants' work in the performance world include Helen Mirren (who was in the Peter Brook company for a while), Yehudi Menuhin, Neil Young, Francis Fisher and Whoopi Goldberg.

I have only sketched in some of Moshe Feldenkrais's extraordinary life experience but you can read about it in much more detail.[9] What I really want to spend time with is his connection with actors and how and why his Method got into the acting world – and in the UK especially.

I began with this first lesson of standing on the hands at the start of the Santa Juan Bautista workshop because this and the other workshops he did for Peter Brook's company form the main point of entry for the Feldenkrais Method into the UK performance world. But what was he aiming to bring out of the actors with this very difficult lesson? Does it mean the Method is just to help actors do clever tricks and gymnastics? It is important to understand that these kind of lessons are not the norm in the Method; in fact, while there are many lessons that are difficult in many ways, this one is considerably more physically challenging than any I have come across. Feldenkrais was given to saying he created conditions for you to learn how to do *the thing you already know, in another way* (which is an idea unpacked later in this book), because being able to make a choice about how to do the simplest of things is so much what an actor needs. So reaching, pushing, pulling, standing, sitting, walking, jumping and so on are the kinds of things we find the lessons addressing more often than standing on your hands and doing the splits.

Frank Wildman told me that some of the workshop was concerned with exploring bird movements which were specifically relevant to *The Conference of the Birds*, but in general it went on being extremely difficult, with all kinds of rolling, including dive-rolling: Feldenkrais asked Yoshi Oida to dive-roll around a stick all the way down the room to illustrate how his centre of gravity was outside himself in this movement. I have heard a little of the way Feldenkrais liked to challenge these actors on a rare (currently unavailable) tape of one of the workshops at Bouffes du Nord in Paris, where Feldenkrais is clearly enjoying himself getting the actors to put one leg out, keep it there unmoving, but then turn towards the leg (*not* away), jump right over it with the other leg, and end up facing the other way. It is relatively easy to do badly but actually pretty difficult to do in the way he is asking (i.e. without moving the extended leg all over the place or dropping it lower). You can find a published version of this lesson amongst those he taught in a street named Alexander Yanai in Tel Aviv, but that was a class he taught for many years and you can find other pretty difficult lessons there too. In the Paris tapes, one or two of the actors are clearly rather good at it, and soon we hear them inventing all sorts of possibilities, like putting a leg on a table and jumping over it, and finding games which Feldenkrais finds very funny. He clearly loves and encourages that kind of the playfulness, and this may be a clue to what he is looking to do in that first lesson too. It is certainly one of the ways all the lessons in the Method work for actors, for as we will see, they require curiosity, spontaneity and creativity either to help solve a difficult puzzle (like that first lesson on the hands) or to find different possibilities at much more accessible levels of physical challenge. These are all qualities that an actor needs to develop too.

The other recordings from the Paris sessions are made up of more accessible lessons – albeit still on the more dynamic side – and anyone who has done much of the Feldenkrais Method would recognise them. So it is not that he only, or even usually, created this kind of challenge for actors. It is possible that he did so in the Santa Juan workshop to be sure he was taking the group (which included many physically adept people like Yoshi Oida and Frank Wildman) into an arena that was unusual enough to grab their attention and ensure that they definitely experienced something novel. This gives us another key element of the Method which is very important for actors, because they need a wide repertoire of possible ways of being. Most lessons in the Method do this in much less dramatic ways, but they still include movements that are reversed or asked for in unusual ways. I love seeing the drama students' faces when they come up to standing after a Feldenkrais lesson and their eyes widen at some feeling of themselves they have simply never had before.

In that handstanding lesson, for example, it's not so important that you can do it all. Just having a go invites you to feel what it is like to reverse your usual way of being: to put the weight down through your arms instead of your legs, to have your head and eyes near the floor instead of high up. Then, if you can do that much, you get to feel what it is like to move your back, chest, pelvis and legs in relation to fixed, weight-bearing arms and shoulders rather than the other way around, so when you come back to your feet with your head upright, you feel a clear difference in the way you stand, and in how and where your shoulders and arms hang – your sense of how you can use them is sometimes surprisingly new. You can see a video online (vimeo.com/25220704) where Frank Wildman does a lesson based on this with a performer – and the young man's face is a picture afterwards: he can't stop grinning and trying out what he can do.

There is also no way you can really do all of this upside-down lesson with physical strength alone. Of course, it takes some strength to support yourself on your hands at all, but it also involves finding out how you can balance in this novel situation; how you can feel where your legs are in the air; how to shift weight; which way to twist so that you can even think of taking a hand away. This also gets to more elements of the Method: how you balance and shift balance; how you operate within gravity and in relation to the ground; how you organise the whole of yourself more skilfully rather than just force or strain in unnecessary ways. These are all essential parts of the learning, whether the lesson is as dramatic as this or apparently simpler – like lifting a leg, reaching with an arm or rolling up to sit.

In this book I will be focusing on just a few of the more accessible lessons, but it is worth knowing that there are very challenging lessons amongst those Feldenkrais created. Always remember that improvement comes not so much from just being able to execute the instructions in the lessons, as from the way you are invited to explore and learn.

Peter Brook liked working with Moshe Feldenkrais because he had a more precise understanding of movement than anyone he knew, but it may also have been because Feldenkrais did not advocate a system with specific ways of doing things.[10] The thinking his Method is built on is rigorous, but it is exploratory in its approach. This is another reason why it is so useful for actors. Actors don't want to have to follow a set of rules or always stick to what is considered 'correct', because it gets in the way of spontaneity and creativity – and because they may want to be able to play all sorts of people who behave and move in all kinds of ways that simply don't follow any rules. I remember Nicholas Hytner, then Artistic Director of the National Theatre, in a seminar on the role of movement directors many years ago saying that he didn't want his actors 'Methoded to death'. Peter Brook may have felt the same. You don't come out of the Feldenkrais Method with a specific way of holding yourself or moving. You don't come out with rules, but you do discover more about yourself and your potential. You do develop skill.

Along with the letter at the start of this chapter, this passage from John Heilpern's book *The Conference of the Birds* about the great trip to Africa gave me a sense of what Peter Brook was responding to in Feldenkrais's work:

> Brook told me that if you watch any cat, it isn't just that his body is so relaxed and expressive. It's something more important than that. A cat actually thinks visibly. If you watch him jump on a shelf, the wish to jump and the action of jumping are one and the same thing. There's no division. A thought animates his whole body. It's in exactly the same way that all Brook's exercises try to train the actor. The actor is trained to become so organically related within himself, he thinks completely with his body. He becomes one sensitive responding whole, like the cat.[11]

For me those last two sentences capture a great deal about the Feldenkrais Method too.

Monika Pagneux

From here I want to travel to another very significant piece of the story which involves the highly gifted movement teacher Monika Pagneux. She met Moshe Feldenkrais at one of his workshops at Peter Brook's centre in Paris in 1975. Her great

facility and understanding as a teacher came from a background that included working with dancer/teacher Mary
Wigman, who in turn was a student of the movement analyst
Rudolf Laban, but Feldenkrais's work was to have a big impact
on her.[12] She never became a trained Feldenkrais practitioner,
but she talked about him a great deal and shared a considerable
amount of his work as part of her wonderful teaching at both
the Jacques Lecoq school and in the years she was teaching
alongside Philippe Gaulier, as well as during the years of teaching on her own that followed. I know because she taught me in
Paris, 1984–6, and like many other UK performers it is through
her I discovered the Feldenkrais Method. Her other students
and their students in turn include many members of the well-
known theatre group Théâtre de Complicité (now Complicite),
and a whole host of other physical-theatre companies and performers that came out of the late 1970s, '80s, '90s, and into this
millennium. Monika has never liked being interviewed about
her work for books or articles so I was unable to persuade her
to talk to me. She feels that movement is an experience that cannot be captured in writing. However, there is a precious
documentary about her work which she was happy to make.[13] I
will discuss this later.

Some Key Feldenkrais Practitioners

Monika's impact on this story is very great, but exposure to
Monika wasn't the only way that the Method arrived in the UK.
The big professional trainings Feldenkrais taught in the USA
from 1973 till his death in 1984 included a number of performers and dancers. Among them was **Garet Newell**, who came
to the UK in the early 1980s. Garet talked to me about how she
started out with an interest in choreography and trained in
modern dance technique with Martha Graham and in the
schools of Merce Cunningham and of José Límon in New York.
She completed her masters in dance at New York University

(1976) and also studied with the influential experimental dance teacher Anna Halprin in San Francisco. In the late 1970s, Garet met John Graham and taught 'Gentle Dance' with him while they were both students in Feldenkrais's Amherst training. Her workshops with John Graham in London introduced her to a number of performers, some of whom would come to her Feldenkrais classes there years later. (Interestingly, back in the early 1970s it was John and Anna who had suggested Frank Wildman attend the Santa Juan Bautista workshop and join the training Feldenkrais taught in San Francisco soon after.)

Garet had already read Feldenkrais's books during her masters, and now in San Francisco she met and had lessons with Feldenkrais practitioner Jerry Karzen. An accident during her masters had left her with pain and difficulty in moving. She told me that, although she had had lessons with very good Alexander teachers (including Walter Carrington on occasions when he came to London) and was intending to study to be an Alexander teacher herself, the lessons with Jerry Karzen went beyond her experience: 'It touched something in me that said this is what I want to learn.' She joined the Amherst training in 1980 and soon after came to the UK to take up an offer to teach at The Open Centre in Central London.

Garet has taught in the UK ever since and has run Professional Practitioner Trainings since 1987, which until very recently were the only ones in existence in the UK. That on its own, taking into account her appeal to performers as one of their own kind, would be enough to qualify her as significant in the development of the Feldenkrais Method in the UK performance world – though there was a very important development in 1987. In that year, along with Christopher Connolly, another graduate of the Amherst training who had come back to the UK, she was invited to the annual International Workshop Festival in London founded by Nigel Jamieson, at which they were asked to teach Feldenkrais as the 'warm-up' and 'wind-down' hours at the beginning and end of every day. Garet told me that she was very impressed with Nigel Jamieson for being aware of the Method at that time, for recognising its value to performers and for taking on something so little known when he could have gone a more well-trodden route. Nigel had been working in physical theatre for many years (in 1985 he won a Greater London Arts Award for his outstanding contribution to the fields of Dance and Physical Theatre). He had also worked with Monika Pagneux in Paris who he describes as 'an immensely wise and sublime teacher' and wanted to bring her along with many others to London 'at a time when there were few chances to study forms other than text-based Western theatre traditions'. He also told me:

> In addition to bringing Monika to London, we were
> keen to programme the work of British-based
> Feldenkrais practitioners, and encourage its integration
> into actor training and preparation in the UK.
> Feldenkrais seemed to offer a wonderful way of
> preparing and balancing the performer's mind and
> body, across a number of disciplines that we promoted.

It was indeed a great thing that he did.

Dick McCaw PhD, who took over the Festival in 1993 and ran it until 2001, recognised the value in what Nigel had introduced and was able to develop it even further. Dick had already co-founded two major theatre companies: the Actors Touring Company in 1978 and the Medieval Players in 1981. He is now an independent researcher and senior lecturer at Royal Holloway, University of London, with many publications to his name. He completed the Professional Feldenkrais practitioner Training with Garet Newell at the same time as I did – in 2007. He said to me that he never even questioned the tradition of the Feldenkrais wind-down at the end of every day during the Workshop Festival ('To me it was a no-brainer, of course we would continue the Feldenkrais!'), but that he could see that:

While this is a valid use of Feldenkrais's work I think that he can offer much more to a sensitive movement artist – he offers us a way of understanding how to connect with another person's movement... My years of difficulty with learning movement has helped me understand the wisdom of Feldenkrais's statement that his Method is not about learning skills, techniques, procedures (though it does involve all three things), it is also learning how to learn.

And so from 1995 he invited Garet Newell to lead two or three day workshops every year the Festival ran. 'I let the teaching stand for itself and let them make meaning out of it,' Garet told me, but she also understands and can respond to the needs and questions of performers and from my experience of her teaching she will have been able to communicate the value of the work for them very effectively. Many actors, directors and movement directors, and even musicians and voice teachers, went through her workshops, taking an awareness of and interest in Feldenkrais into their own performance worlds. These included the renowned voice and singing teacher Venice Manley, with whom Garet also taught later. Some of them also went on to train as Feldenkrais teachers many years later.

Dick McCaw also began to offer a platform at the International Workshop Festival to three other Feldenkrais teachers establishing themselves in the field: Scott Clark, Andrew Dawson and Jos Houben, all graduates of the first two UK trainings. **Scott Clark** now led the wind-downs. He already had a considerable reputation as a dancer and as a dance teacher. He was a co-founder of the Siobhan Davies Dance Company and taught the company for its first six years. Since qualifying from the first UK Feldenkrais training in 1990, he has become one of the most proactive Feldenkrais practitioners in the UK, making an enormous difference to its profile amongst dancers, performers and the general public alike. He has been an important figure in developing the UK Feldenkrais Guild and its website and was its chair for many years. He has also taught on Professional Practitioner trainings for a number of years internationally, and now runs a new professional training in London. His private practice and his well-known classes and workshops attract many dancers and performers, as well as very diverse members of the general public.

Andrew Dawson taught his first public workshops during the Festival. His original training was in mime and dance, and he also studied with Jacques Lecoq, Philippe Gaulier and Monika Pagneux. He was on the second Feldenkrais training in the UK along with Jos, both qualifying in 1994. This is what he said to me about how he and Jos Houben first encountered the Method:

> Jos and I came to the Method together. We were
> attending a directors' workshop with Philippe Gaulier
> in Paris in the summer of 1987. Monika Pagneux was
> teaching the mornings and did these funny movements
> that made my arm get longer. By the end of the six
> weeks she had revealed that it came from Mr Feldi.

(This sounds exactly like my own experience with Monika back in 1984; I think it expresses very nicely how so many of us first came across the Method.) Since then Andrew has juggled his work as a Feldenkrais teacher with his ongoing career in performance, making his own unique contributions to the Feldenkrais world through his direction and movement direction (in places that include the Met Opera in New York, English National Opera and the Bristol Old Vic in the UK), and through his richly imaginative workshops for performers in the UK and the US. In addition, his talk on Ted Med, his beautifully crafted videos for the Feldenkrais Guild made with his son, Roman, and his own very interesting performance pieces and collaborations (that sometimes incorporate and always embody the work) continue to inspire.

Jos Houben trained with Lecoq and was a founder member of Complicite. He also worked as collaborator, performer and movement director on many shows with many companies and performers in the UK from the 1980s onwards. Jos led several weekend workshops at the International Workshop Festival and a week-long one in 1996. He has been the movement teacher at L'École International de Théâtre Jacques Lecoq in Paris for many years now, no doubt inspiring many with his playful and profoundly enabling approach. He also still performs.

It can clearly be said that when the Method first arrived in the UK, most performers and directors encountered it first either through Monika Pagneux or Garet Newell and the other Feldenkrais teachers at the International Workshop Festival. From these beginnings the work has spread to include teachers at quite a number of universities, acting, music and dance schools, as well as practitioners who work with professionals and/or bring the work to their movement direction, performance work and theatre-making. It is difficult to include all of the practitioners now in this field, as there are an ever-growing number doing good and important work that continues to spread awareness of the Method, but I must mention four or five others from the first two trainings in this country who made an impact on the performance world.

Maggy Burrowes, who qualified on the first training in 1990, will reappear in my chapter on voice because she came to the Feldenkrais Method as a singer looking for a way to work with voice. Her subsequent studies with Alison Bagnell and Jo Estill give her a unique skill set, and her VocalDynamix and Embodied Voice courses continue to attract both actors and singers (although her practice is not only focused on the voice, and she leads workshops on many themes). Maggy has worked with several performance groups, including The Festival Shakespeare Company, Re:Action Theatre and dance company CandoCo. She worked with The Right Size on several occasions, including during the development of *The Play What I Wrote* – a celebration of Morecambe and Wise – which debuted at the Liverpool Playhouse in 2001 and transferred successfully to the West End.

Shelagh O'Neill PhD, who also qualified in 1990, has a flourishing practice in the West of England, teaches workshops abroad and teaches on professional trainings. Her interest is not in performance per se, but in using the Feldenkrais Method to enable people to develop a clear sense of self. For performers, this is the foundation they work from. She has worked with, among others, string players and singers in the Welsh National Opera, students from Bristol Old Vic Theatre School, and performers from Kneehigh, and has touched many more through her teaching at Fooltime and Circomedia in Bristol in the 1990s.

Gunther Bisges teaches on many professional trainings internationally and still maintains a faithful following in his native Germany (where he created a series of classes for German TV), but he has his main practice in the UK now. I know from my own work with him that he enjoys working with performers and loves to find the playful edge of the Method. He has worked as a guest teacher for the Laban Centre, London, as well as the Performing Arts Academies in Munich, Hong Kong and the Royal Dramaten in Stockholm – and at one of his workshops not so long ago I recognised most of the movement department of one of the other top drama schools in London.

Thomas Kampe, Richard Cave and Libby Worth are exceptions in my list as they didn't qualify until 2003, 1998 and 2011 respectively; however, they have in different ways been at the vanguard of the shift of the Method into the performance departments of universities and colleges.

Working as a team, **Richard Cave PhD** (Emeritus Professor) and **Libby Worth PhD** have developed courses in the Department of Drama and Theatre at Royal Holloway, University of London, which have included Feldenkrais since the late 1990s. Richard Cave also gave group and one-to-one Feldenkrais lessons at the Royal Shakespeare Company from 2003 to 2014 as part of the Artist Development Programme, instituted by Michael Boyd, both to enable skills and to help actors engage comfortably with the demands of particular roles. He now works regularly with a number of physical-theatre companies, including Theatre Ad Infinitum, and teaches Feldenkrais classes for Shakespeare's Globe on the actor training programmes they deliver for the Guthrie Theatre (Minnesota) and the Department of Theatre Arts at Rutgers (New Jersey).

Libby trained with Anna Halprin and John Graham (the same influential dance teachers Garet Newell and Frank Wildman worked with). She discovered Feldenkrais through them and through Norma Leistiko, a long-term member of the San Francisco Dancers Workshop, who taught on Anna Halprin's training programmes. Libby says that Norma:

> taught anatomy through drawing and Feldenkrais lessons, with breaks for dancing to loud music and very often with classical music playing in the background. She was a wonderful teacher who made the training her own.

Back in the UK, Libby took part in some of Garet Newell's earliest classes, and many years later her work with Richard Cave finally convinced her to take the training to become a Feldenkrais practitioner.

Thomas Kampe PhD has a dance background in the post-Laban tradition, Release and Contact Improvisation. He is important in this story because he has taught so extensively in many drama schools since the 1980s and has been at the forefront of the move into higher education – at Chichester, London Metropolitan and Bath Spa universities. He continues to put together interesting research projects around Feldenkrais and somatic-informed performance, impacting on many students and practitioners alike.

It's also important to say that a number of performers or directors who have come across the Method have done a considerable amount to spread the work, even though they are not actually themselves practitioners. Director/performer **Annabel Arden** comes to mind: she studied extensively with

Monika Pagneux and did part of the Feldenkrais training with Garet Newell. Also significant here is director, theatre-maker and teacher **John Wright**, who discovered the Method originally through Christopher Connolly and who also worked with Monika and did some workshops with Garet. Annabel was a founder member of Complicite and is well known for her work in theatre and opera. John founded Trestle Theatre and co-founded Told by an Idiot, and has used clowning and masks of many kinds in his teaching and directing for many years. Indeed he has taught, directed and worked with a huge swathe of the physical-theatre world, and his book *Why Is That So Funny?* is widely read (he is writing a second as I write this). He has been and still is a great advocate for the Method and attends weekly classes. Although not a Feldenkrais practitioner himself, his warm-ups and ways of approaching movement are strongly influenced by the work, and many a performer, inspired by John, has gone looking for a class, a workshop or a practitioner – some have even ended up training as practitioners themselves. I have the pleasure of teaching with John on occasion these days, and it was because of a workshop he asked me to teach at the Actors Centre that this book was commissioned. I know there are very many more spreading the word in their own way.

As I have said, these days there are Feldenkrais teachers like myself in a growing number of drama, dance and music schools as well as several universities in the UK. A number of us also work with professionals in the field of performance. Many are doing excellent work and I apologise for not listing everyone. Some of them will still crop up later in the book or in the 'resources' section where I have quoted them or pointed you towards their writing or research. Relatively speaking, we are still a select bunch, but Garet Newell's two current trainings and the newer London training organised by Scott Clark, combined with those practitioners who come back to the UK after training abroad, are beginning to make more and more of an impact.

Many thanks to Garet Newell, Frank Wildman, Dick McCaw, Maggy Burrowes, Andrew Dawson, Shelagh O'Neill, Scott Clark, Richard Cave, Libby Worth, Thomas Kampe, John Wright and Nigel Jamieson for talking to me, sending me biographical information, making suggestions or approving what I have written, and to Francois Combeau for making it possible for me to hear the tapes of Moshe Feldenkrais teaching at Bouffes Du Nord in Paris.

Dr Moshe Feldenkrais teaching at Amherst in the USA in the early 1980s
© International Feldenkrais Federation Archive

Part 1

'When You Know What You Do,
You Can Do What You Want'

1a. Knowing What You Do

Patterns and Habits

'They said they didn't see me as vulnerable enough to read for the part. It's ridiculous. Of course I can play a vulnerable character! It's called *acting*. That's my job!'

Maybe. Maybe not.

No one starts as a blank piece of paper on which to write any character, and no one can ever truly become one however hard they try. That is not as controversial as it may initially sound to some. As the renowned teacher Jacques Lecoq said: 'Of course there is no such thing as absolute and universal neutrality. It is merely a temptation.'[14] We will get to the uses of the study of neutrality (which Lecoq made famous) in Part 3, but first it is important to acknowledge this: we are unique individuals and recognisably so. The mould got broken every time. We each have our own unique expression of an individual genome; we went through a childhood that no one else did; we have had (and continue to have) our own experiences of life; we learnt our own way of standing, turning, bending, reaching, walking, thinking, breathing – no one else does it exactly the same. Not just our genes and structure but our many stories have shaped and continue to shape our very fabric, and to fashion the very specific patterns and habits of doing, responding and being that we all have. We cannot simply strip it all away.

And that is not necessarily a bad thing for actors. In a sense it's a gift: this is material you can use. Some of the patterns and habits you have will be the reason you get the part as well as the reason you don't; they might even be the reason that the audience will (or already do!) turn out or switch on in their millions to see you. But, of course, not all patterns: some of them you may wish you could change so that you could do something differently – or just better. Some of them will be getting in the way without you even knowing. Many of your patterns and habits are shiftable, changeable, expandable, variable – you aren't necessarily stuck with all of them as they are for ever – but if you want to do anything differently you need to know what you are doing in the first place. You will take these patterns and habits of yours onstage, in front of the camera and when you walk through the door for an audition. It's important to be very clear from the beginning that this is what you are working with, and to appreciate that one thing that can really enhance your acting is to know as much as you can about the very particular patterns and habits that are currently yours. If you don't, there is less you will be able to do with or about them: your choices will be constrained in ways that you may not even recognise. Becoming aware of your patterns of moving and being at ever-deepening levels and in progressively finer detail, as well as learning to expand and develop them, are skills the Feldenkrais Method enables particularly well. It is a way of becoming freer from the tyranny of habits in a way that, in my experience, works beautifully with Lecoq's idea of neutrality, not against. These are some significant reasons for an actor to practise the Method and a great place to start.

How Much Do You Know About What You Do?

Take a really simple everyday action like walking. Do you know what you are doing when you walk? It's actually a huge question as they still (as far as I am aware) haven't been able to build a robot that can truly walk like a human being because it is so complex. But ask yourself just a bit of it:

What do you do to bring your right leg forward? Do you twist the pelvis? (If so, in what direction?) Does the hip go up/down/neither? Do you bend sideways in the ribs? (If so, to which side?) What does your right shoulder do? Lift/drop? Move forward/backward/neither? Does your lower back lengthen/shorten/neither? How is your breastbone involved? What does your head do? Where do you look with your eyes? What part of your foot (exactly) is the last to leave the floor? How does the weight shift on your other foot? And do you do the same when you bring the other leg through? (Extremely unlikely – but what's the difference?)

That's just a few questions, I could think of many more. I'm not really expecting you to have that much of an idea unless you happen to be an expert: if you had any answers you did well.

How You Developed Those Patterns

Before we go further, it's important to unpack a little of the background to the rather bald initial assertions I have made. Important because, as we will see, this is fundamental to the Feldenkrais Method and it's really very interesting for actors. I don't want to get bogged down in the detail of the scientific evidence for how we learn, so I am going to stick to what we really need to understand the Method, and to elucidate what you are working with as an actor. I have included references and there is suggested Further Reading (in the Appendix) if you want to explore this area further.

To understand how you acquired the patterns and habits you have, and to appreciate their depth and complexity, we need to go back in time. When you were born your nervous system was not all wired up as it is now. The basic life functions that involve movement were wired up – breathing and circulation of the blood, sucking (milk), digestion, excretion (albeit some of them, like digestion, needed a bit of practice to work well!) – but most musculoskeletal movement was random and you could not control it. It usually takes up to fifteen months of extraordinary learning to be able to move around on the floor, use your hands with basic dexterity, stand and ultimately be mobile on two legs. And the learning goes on for the whole of your life. Compare that to any other creature that is born already wired in such a way that it can run, slide, hop, fly, swim, in a fraction of the time – sometimes pretty much immediately after birth – or it will starve, get left behind or become someone else's lunch. Human beings have to go through a lengthy process of development. It's not some pre-programmed process that simply unfolds in us over a specific time frame either. Rather, we develop through our interaction with others and the world: a very complex, personal process within a specific environment.[15] Let's see an example...

I have one such moment caught very beautifully on camera from a project I did filming babies for the first fifteen months of their lives. In this moment the baby (two months old) is lying on his back on a mat and I have placed a toy strategically on the floor where he can see it, somewhere a little bit away from one side of his head. At this point all this baby can do is wave his arms and legs in a kind of random movement, but he can track with his eyes, focus on things nearby, and turn his head intentionally. The random movement of his arms eventually means that he hits the toy. His attention is caught. He has felt himself touch the toy and out of the corner of his eye has seen the toy wobble. In short, something he has done has made something happen in the world, and he has felt and recognised it. *Exciting!* He wants to do it again. You can see it. He has turned his head and is looking at the toy and the waving becomes a little more frantic. But he cannot control his arm to make it touch the toy again. Then suddenly, accidentally (but maybe a little less accidentally this time?): bingo. He hits the toy. It wobbles. He is still looking at it. Everything is going manically now because he can't limit his movements, prioritise or direct them. Everything is engaged, legs, arms, all waving. Once more: bingo. This time the toy falls over. *Wow!* And again. And again. And gradually you can see how the randomness is becoming a little less random, a little more directed. Head, eye, hand are beginning to coordinate to make something happen that he wants to happen. He is learning. His system is recognising the sensation of those movements, seeking to reproduce the parts of the movement that go towards achieving his intention, and eliminating the parts of the movement that are not effective or useful. Through this process, he begins to learn to direct his hand and arm more and more not just to hit but even to grab the toy. *And get it into his mouth!* Over the next few weeks he develops and refines. He adds other new skills he is learning with his foot and pelvis that enable him to shift his weight a bit so his arm can reach better or he can reach with both arms. He establishes a useful pattern of rolling, reaching and grabbing that he can repeat and repeat. The more the pattern is repeated, the more it is wired in.[16]

This very creative process in a child leads to many repeatable discoveries, and in so doing 'ripens' the nervous system; prioritising some connections, pruning away others; developing how the child moves, acts, responds; establishing patterns of movement, expectation and behaviour specific to that child created through its interaction with the world. Renowned developmental expert (and Feldenkrais practitioner) Esther Thelen did some excellent research in this area, and wrote most elegantly about how the child's abilities and sense of self emerge together through this interaction with the world: a combination of impulse, intention, accident, experiment, improvisation and discovery. Interestingly, Esther Thelen compares this kind of learning to the activity of a jazz performer,[17] but we could equally compare it to that of an actor. I said this description would contain the fundamentals of the Feldenkrais Method – well, there it is right there: that creative process of organic learning that we all engaged in as children (and still do) is at its heart which, in turn, links directly to an actor's process too.

But all in good time.

To go back to where we were: this process of development defines us as astonishing learners and extremely adaptable to our surroundings, but that brings with it difficulties as well as advantages. Shout at this same child when he reaches for the toy and he will flinch. His stomach muscles will contract, his arms will be thrown outwards, he will go into the 'startle response' or 'Moro reflex', which is one of the few things deeply wired in from the start.[18] Do that every time he goes to reach for the toy and it will begin to affect his pattern of reaching. Very likely he will no longer want to reach for the toy at all. But if he does, that glorious, pleasurable, lengthening movement he was developing is likely to be compromised by the anticipation of danger. As he starts to lengthen to reach for the toy, his system will be contradicting the movement already by contracting in fearful anticipation. What happens if this becomes wired in? It is likely to become an unconscious part of his pattern of reaching unless he has enough other kinds of experience to teach him something different again.[19] Moshe Feldenkrais called it 'cross-motivation',[20] and we will come back to it. But learning can be affected in many ways. What if there was no toy there and nothing to catch his interest? What if he was kept for very long periods of time in a buggy or a bouncy chair? What if he had to compete for that toy with other children all the time? His sensory-motor learning might well be different again.

And in this way we are the sum of our learning. Watch two children over time and you will see how differently they shape up: what space they are in; what is around them; what they are allowed to do; the family or people they are interacting with; those people's involvement, lack of involvement, expectations, warmth, coldness, desires, interests; what the results of the child's explorations and attempts are; how safe the child is to try things out or not to – it all has its effect on what and how they learn in complicated, profound and detailed ways, that layer up and integrate and are not easily teased apart, analysed or simply codified. This is how we piece together and wire-in our first ways of operating in the world. And we don't stop learning at fifteen months. We go on all our life learning different skills; not learning others; giving things up; discovering others; getting frightened or nervous in some areas of life or developing confidence in others; rushing excitedly into some activities, shunning others; wanting to be seen in one way and not another, to be acceptable to this group and not seen as part of that; experiencing trauma, difficulty, upset, comfort and pleasure in different degrees and ways; learning, relearning. All of it creates patterns of behaviour that are held in our nervous system and show up in the base level of tension (tonus), timing and organisation of our skeletal neuromuscular system, i.e. the way we stand, breathe, shake hands, reach, laugh, walk, sit. And when you come into the room, onstage or on to set, you bring all that with you whether you like it or not. Because you are a human being. And that is fine. But you are not and never will be a blank sheet of paper on which to draw a character – and nor do you need to be. The really important question is, 'How much do you actually know about what you are bringing with you? Do you know what you do?' Because if you don't know much, what kind of choice can you make about it? How can you improve your skills or start to work with what you could do differently?

Do You Really Know What You Do?

Of course, all of us know something of this, and you more than most probably because (I assume if you are reading this) you are an actor or have an interest in acting, and it is an actor's job to embody someone else with their different patterns and habits. Besides, even a child knows it's fun to point out or copy someone else because they do something in a different way; every teenager knows there is a cool way and a less cool way to walk. But look again at the baby's behaviour: we often forget or don't really appreciate just how deep that goes, just how complex and layered it is, the amount of tiny detail involved, how little we are aware of our own patterns and just what they say about us.

It still surprises me how many young actors turn up at drama school and are shocked at how much time movement classes take up. I also notice how often experienced actors lose their curiosity about themselves and are happy to ignore movement work other than some fitness training, and only rediscover it if they get injured or develop chronic pain. Indeed, if you are an experienced actor you may be thinking that the Feldenkrais Method isn't for you, that you know enough about yourself and your patterns of movement already. But, with respect, no one does. There is too much to know. You may have worked long enough to have got into some ruts, which means you may need this work as much or more than a student. This is a question you can answer to great advantage whatever age you are and however experienced, because we can learn at deeper levels throughout our lives. We can always improve. You can take that as depressing or exciting. As a Feldenkrais practitioner, I find it exhilarating and fascinating because *if you know what you do, you can do what you want.* Well, maybe not entirely, but if you don't know what you do, you can't make much of a start. Or at least we can say: the more you know what you do, the more you increase your possibilities.

The Stories Our Patterns Tell

It's especially important for actors because your patterns are on show, so everyone *else* will know things about you, or think they do, as soon as they see you. They will recognise your habits whether they realise it or not, and they will make assumptions about you and create stories about you, right or wrong, whether they mean to or not. Because we are wired up to do that too. A baby needs to recognise its mum or whoever is feeding it (apparently it can do that by smell from three days old). It needs to recognise differences in facial – and later whole body – signals, and it does that from a surprisingly young age.[21] I would put good money on you being able to recognise a good friend, close relative or lover at the top of the road or pick them out at the train station, even if you can't see their face and they are with a bunch of other people dressed very like them. You will also know if it's *not* them too – even if the person you are looking at looks, and is dressed, just like them. Because, whether you can articulate any of it or not, something in you knows in real detail exactly how they stand, the precise rhythm of their walk, the manner with which they sweep the hair away from their face, the timing and angle to the turn of their head. And they would recognise you for all the same reasons.

When you meet someone new it is important to have some idea about them too. You will have an innate sense of what they are like and whether you trust them or not. But there is nothing mystical about it, you are just picking up all sorts of cues and patterns, comparing it to experiences you have had previously and things you already know about people who have similar or contrasting patterns – quite possibly without even realising you are doing it. You may be totally wrong, but you are busily engaged in doing it. Conversely, other people will be doing that with you all the time. *Especially when you turn up onstage or in a film.* You can never entirely control what other people think, but you can have a good go at creating something that you hope communicates the story you want. But to do that you have to know something about what you are doing in the first place. If you don't know that, I repeat, you haven't got much possibility of doing anything with it.

The Stories People Tell Without Telling

Go and sit in a café or at the bus station or in the park, or wherever you like that's public and where you can do so without being too easily noticed (and punched!). Just watch someone for a while and notice what assumptions you make about them and why. What's the story you have about them? You'll have one. Or several. And they won't be random. You will have reasons if you ask yourself where you are getting them from. What is it about their physicality – not just their clothes, age, hairstyle, accessories – that gives you clues?

Then watch someone and try not to make any stories or have any assumptions about them. Make yourself watch them for a good five minutes. It's pretty hard not to have *any* idea about them at all.

An example: a young actress has a slight tendency to sink in the top ribs at the front just under the collarbone. It makes her look a little round-shouldered. It gives her a slightly unconfident, vulnerable, self-protected look. Surprisingly, a director casts her as Lady Macbeth. She is very excited. It's unusual casting for her, but the director is interested in exploring a less traditional, more fragile Lady M. It's an example of her unconscious pattern transmitting something that gets her the job, so it's not a bad thing altogether. However, there are moments when the director does want her to find a flash of real power. 'You need to really take your ground at this point. Stand tall,' she says to the actress. The actress cranks herself up by lifting her lower ribs at the front and arching her lower back more, which just makes her look a little chesty and tight and cut off in the waist. 'No, no. Pull your shoulders back,' says the director. The actress duly pulls her shoulders back. Her collarbones pull tight across the front of her chest, her back is stiff and her throat is compressed. The top ribs are still sinking and it's hard to talk properly. 'No no. Relax more!' the director tells her. She sags. Internally, the director begins to question the wisdom of her casting.

The thing is that our actress can't feel enough of what she is doing to learn to modify it, and the director can't help her. She may have been told all the way through drama school that her 'posture isn't good', and may even have done quite a lot of exercises to improve aspects of it, but she still doesn't really know what it is she is doing. Opening the top ribs is not the same as pulling the shoulders back and it's not the same as arching the lower back, but as she can't feel what her ribs and shoulders have got to do with each other, or what either have to do with her pelvis, she can't begin to explore those relationships and find anything new. Until that point it will affect her casting and, perhaps more importantly, her range and skill within that casting.

So now I am hoping we have established that you have deeply complex patterns and habits and that, as an actor, you could always benefit from being more aware of them. The next question is, how does the Feldenkrais Method help you do that? And no doubt the question after that is going to be, 'And what can I do with them and about them?' Because as we have seen, not all habits are useful (as with this young actress and with that poor baby we imagined earlier who learnt to contract every time he tried to lengthen and reach), and because you want to be able to have more control over what you do and how you come across. Ultimately, you want to find some new/different possibilities to increase your range. Well, as it happens, that is exactly what the Method can enable you to do better.

But first things first.

Some preliminaries for all the Feldenkrais lessons in the book:

- Find yourself somewhere warm enough and/or wear something that won't let you get too cold from lying still.

- If you know you find the floor too hard to lie on (on your back), get a mat or blanket or make sure you have a nice carpet under you. But not a mattress or the sofa – if it is too soft, you sink in too much to be able to feel the things I'm going to ask.

- If your head is uncomfortably tilted back when you lie on your back, put a folded towel or blanket under it, but not so much that you push your chin too far forward or into your throat.

- If your back is very arched and feels uncomfortable when you lie on your back with your legs long, roll up a blanket and put it under your knees to keep them a bit bent (usually, the bigger the roller, the more it takes the arch out of your back). Or bend your knees and plant your feet (you won't get the same information with your feet in this position, though), or just do it for a short while and do some more later. Or don't do it at all!

- If anything actually hurts, *stop*. Get up. Change position. Do something to relieve it. Pain is a signal that your system reckons what you are doing isn't safe for you. Listen to it and act on it. For some people, just lying on the floor is problematic. I'm not there so I can't know how it is for you, and even if I was it is part of the Method that you begin to listen to yourself and learn to look after yourself.

- You might even want to record the lessons so you can listen rather than have to handle the book at the same time. You can then switch the recording on and off for pauses as required. The lessons vary in length and will take anything from about 5–45 minutes.

Lesson 1: Basic Awareness

Earlier, I asked you to see if you knew all sorts of things about how you walk. It's actually extremely complex to have even a half-accurate answer to that. So here we will go right back to something much simpler: *How do you lie on the floor?* I'm serious. Most Feldenkrais classes start with some version of this and keep coming back to it to feel what's changing as the lesson progresses. Everyone lies on the floor differently, and because you are lying down you have plenty of sensory information from your contact with the ground to help you feel how you are doing it.

Lie on your back. Legs long if you can. Take your attention into yourself. Listen in. Ask yourself: which parts of you lean on the floor most?

Probably somewhere in your pelvis for a start. But where? To the left, the right, higher, lower? Is the pressure comfortable or uncomfortable? Is it all in one place or spread? It is unlikely to be bang in the middle and totally evenly spread: no one is completely symmetrical. If I had a pound for every time someone comes into my studio and tells me they have been told their pelvis is 'out of alignment' I would be a very rich woman, because everyone's is. It's a just a question of how, how much and whether the person can function effectively. So, in what way is your pelvis asymmetrical? You will find the answer if you listen carefully enough.

How about the back of the ribs? Because that's the next place that will probably lean most on the floor. But again, where? If the pelvis is asymmetrical, chances are your chest will be too, though not necessarily in the same way. What presses most? Up near your neck? Lower down your back? Left? Right? It may be hard to tell, depending on how easy you find it to listen in. Listening/feeling is a skill that takes time to develop. You may have it already or you may need to do this a lot to develop it. But everyone can improve and notice finer and finer details.

How about your shoulders? This might be easier. Does one feel closer to the ground or just different in some way?

Your head? Does it lean higher on the back of your skull or lower? Left? Right? Probably one ear is closer to the ground than the other. One ear might be closer to one shoulder than the other too. It's not always easy to tell but have a go. Touch your ears if you need to: measure the distance with your hands.

In between these places that lean heavily are other places in your back that either lean less or don't touch at all.

Your lower back. It arches when you stand. It should do. But lying on the floor it can let go of some of the work involved in arching; it can lengthen and come closer to the floor. It might even touch, but often not. Can you get a sense of how long, how high the arch in your back is? It might even be different on the right side and the left. It's harder to get a sense of the places for which you don't have the sensory feedback from contact with the floor. You have to develop your proprioceptive skills, i.e. your ability to feel yourself (see Part 1b for an explanation) – but you can do it. *The other place is your neck.* That is unlikely to touch. But you may still be able to get a sense of how steep or gentle the arch in your neck is by feeling where it starts in your back and where your head leans.

Then how about your legs? Your right and left leg will not be the same, I can promise you. The differences may be small or large. Listen to your heels and notice if the place they lean is different – more on the inside or outside? You may then find that the same is true for the whole of your leg. How much of your leg touches? Somewhere in the calf, probably, but behind the knee and behind the ankle there are usually gaps unless you have the leg really on its side, and sometimes the gap behind the knee can extend a long way up the thigh. How wide apart do you have your legs?

Arms? Do you have your hands palm up, down, on the side? What parts of the arms touch? What is the difference between them? How far away from your side do you like to have them? Maybe you haven't even put them on the ground but somewhere on your torso. Your choice won't be random. It will be what feels comfortable or familiar – unless you have been taught a specific way that you feel is 'correct' (which for now you should abandon so you can learn about yourself instead).

By now you may be feeling quite lopsided and weird. Welcome to the real world! This is how we are. Maybe you feel curious and interested, or maybe it's frustratingly difficult to feel what is going on at all. If so, don't give up. It takes time to learn a skill and it may get easier later on or if you find a class. So then, what do we do with this? Can we do anything to feel different/better/more even? Yes, of course. But that's to come. This is just for starters in order to have a go at feeling something of how you actually are. So for now, stand up and see how you feel in standing. Maybe the same as before. Maybe heavier, lighter, taller, shorter, with more weight on this foot, more on the other, more balanced or just inexplicably not quite the same.

Even just doing something as simple as this and not moving at all may make standing and moving a different experience, as all the patterns you began to notice on the floor are present in everything you do. But, of course, doing something with them is going to take us a great deal further...

1b. Learning to Do What You Want

In the previous section we looked at how we all have our own personal way of moving and being, which we have learnt and developed since childhood and which we inevitably bring on to the stage or set. I talked about how a child learns to move as wiring up the nervous system: the cells that 'fire' together 'wire' together, creating habitual firing patterns. The more we use those patterns, the stronger the connections become. If we stop using a pattern the connections weaken and can even fall away.[22] We have talked about learning as pruning connections and ripening the nervous system too. I suggested that the Feldenkrais Method is not about attempting to eradicate these habits or 'correct' them because they are part of what makes us *us*, but that as actors (and indeed as people) it is important to be aware that this is the case. At the same time, it is important to know there are other possibilities, and that how we are does not have to be entirely fixed. The Feldenkrais Method gives us a way of exploring those habits. It enables us to become more aware of what we are doing and to develop a greater variety of possible patterns ready and available for our use: a kind of rewiring and sometimes a reawakening of connections we once had and have lost. How does it happen?

The Sixth Sense: Proprioception and the Kinaesthetic Sense

In Lesson 1: Basic Awareness, all we did was a scan. But it's likely that you discovered things that were either new to you or were things you sort of knew but which became clearer because you spent some time paying attention to them in a structured way. It might have been difficult in places or all together. It depends what kind of facility you have for feeling what you do already. But this is a key skill that the Feldenkrais Method enables you to develop through a wide palate of movement as well. You stayed still to make it easier as a starting point and because simply lying like that will become, over time, a kind of reference point for you to return to, to see what has changed. There are a number of reasons for many Feldenkrais lessons taking place lying down, but one reason is so that you can have the sensory information from your contact with it. In this instance, noticing the very particular ways you distribute your weight and how you place your limbs helps you feel how each part of you habitually responds to lying on the floor. It may not be the same after a lesson, part of a lesson, or a series of lessons. Over time you will find this a very eloquent feedback tool for noticing differences in yourself. However, there is also the need to use your 'sixth sense', and that will become an important player in how you learn as you go on – so I need to delve into it a bit.

By sixth sense I don't mean anything telepathic or extra-sensory. I am referring to 'proprioception' or the 'kinaesthetic' sense. It is probably left out of the traditional canon of five because it is not a sense that directly enables you to perceive the outside world; instead it enables you to perceive yourself. It involves the extremely important part of the nervous system that gives you information about yourself – what your joints are doing, where your bones are positioned in relation to each other and in space, the tension level in the muscles, and the level of stretch in the tendons and feedback from the skin.[23] If you didn't have it you wouldn't be able to move or even to stand up easily: your nervous system needs this feedback constantly so that it can activate, inhibit and adjust the work in the musculature to enable you to remain upright or do anything. Most of the time it operates unconsciously, but if you pay attention you can bring it more into the foreground, becoming a crucial tool for learning.

Feldenkrais practitioner and performer Andrew Dawson has done some extremely interesting work with a man called Ian Waterman who came to lack this sixth sense. He taught himself to function by getting the information about his body in other ways, for example, by sight. He had to be sure he was not still standing when the lights went down in the cinema or theatre or he was likely to just fall over. When he woke in the morning he had no 'sense' of himself lying in bed. He painstakingly taught himself how to do all the ordinary things people take for granted, like stand, walk or shake hands, by providing himself with other ways of getting feedback, such as watching himself do it. In Andrew's very powerful performance piece, *The Articulate Hand*, there is extraordinary and very moving footage of Ian trying to light a match with his eyes closed, in which he has to resort to his mouth to try and have some sense of this box and how to handle it.[24] More commonly people lose proprioception in their feet: a kind of neuropathy that can be a side effect of chemotherapy or statins. A member of my family lost the conductivity in just one nerve to the leg/foot. It was a sensory not a motor nerve, but he began shuffling and eventually became mostly wheelchair-bound: the loss of feedback from his leg in movement meant he simply could not use it sufficiently to walk.

Proprioception/The Kinaesthetic Sense

Close your eyes and hold your hand in front of your face. There is a sense in which you can still 'see' it with your eyes closed, isn't there? Move your hand slowly around your head until it is at the back of your head. You can still 'see' it, can't you? And you might well be able to 'see' how much your fingers are curling or how open the palm is and how your fingers are spaced. That is proprioception: you are not experiencing your hand by touching it with any part of yourself or by touching something else or by seeing it, but only through your kinaesthetic sense. That is what Ian didn't have. Can you imagine not having that sense now?

So when discussing this aspect of movement, we often use the term 'the sensory/motor loop'. And as we have seen, the motor part of your nervous system is not very effective without the sensory component. When you move, it is not just a specific set of muscles doing the job. Your nervous system has to execute your intention through an entire pattern of activity that recalibrates your balance, allows for weight-shift and support, and readjusts everything involved; and it needs to have the information about how all those things are in order to fire the appropriate patterns to adjust any of it. All the time there is sensory information going back into the system reporting on how this action is going, so that motor adjustments can be made as necessary to continue to execute the intention as effectively as possible. That information is coming from the visual system and the vestibular (balance) system in the middle ear, as well as the proprioceptive information we are talking about here, and it all needs coordinating. It's an extraordinary job[25] – and often we only know how extraordinary when we lose part of it, so something everyday, like putting a forkful of food into your mouth or taking a step, becomes a mountain of impossibility to negotiate.

Some of that neural firing is also anticipatory, i.e. your system prepares itself for what it *expects* to feel from previous experience of similar actions, and then it may have to make a sudden adjustment if it's wrong. For example, when you pick up a stage prop that looks like a heavy brick but turns out to be made of polystyrene, your arm shoots up because it was pre-programmed for something heavy but suddenly has something light to deal with instead. Or that weird feeling when you are walking downstairs and expect another step down that isn't there. Or answer this: what is one of the worst kinds of ground to run on? How about uneven grassland where the grass is just too long to see what's coming? The unevenness isn't the whole problem, it's the not being able to see what's coming. All the time you are hitting higher or lower parts of the ground you didn't expect, and the muscles in your legs were not pre-programmed for. It's a horrible, jarring experience. I know it well.

So if you want to work with your movement patterns, it's not all about 'doing'. It's about improving the quality of the sensory input and the ways you anticipate the movement, so that the motor system can do its job more effectively. That's why there is so much in the Feldenkrais Method about paying attention to your sensations and noticing what you are doing. It is evidence-based,[26] but it is also common sense. How many times have you tried to learn something in a sport or on an instrument and heard the teacher say, 'No, you are doing X with your arm and you need to do Y!' and you simply have no idea what they mean because you are sure you are doing Y? You may even be cross with them for saying you aren't doing Y! Then suddenly you have an 'aha' moment when you can feel that your arm is doing X; you feel it very clearly and you can feel that X is not in fact Y, and so you are then able to feel what it would be to change it to Y. It means paying attention to what you feel. It may take some reinforcing, and you may go backwards and forwards with it, but you are on the way to making an improvement. That's the interplay of sensory and motor which makes up the sensory/motor loop.

Sensing Differences: Improving Nuance

It turns out, therefore, that improving the sensory part of the sensory/motor loop is crucial for movement, so paying attention to what we can feel lies at the heart of learning or relearning to move – which is why it also lies at the heart of the Feldenkrais Method.

To be a little clearer: what we are sensing are differences between one movement and another; one way of doing things and another; between movement X and movement Y with the arm. Until you can distinguish between them, you can't make a choice between them. Furthermore, finer degrees of sensing difference are needed for finer degrees of skill and finesse. A cellist who cannot hear the difference between a note that is true and one that is a tiny bit flat or sharp will play their piece more or less out of tune, and may not learn to play in tune at all because they will not know that it could be or needs to be different. But a cellist who can hear the difference will learn to play in tune because they will always hear when they need to make an adjustment to the note. Moreover, a cellist who can hear different qualities of sound – sweet, fierce, gentle, passionate – and feel the difference in what they can do to create them in the way they use their arm/self to bow – e.g. with just a little more or less pressure, length or attack of the bow – will have greater degrees of difference and so modulation and nuance available to them. And in the same way the finer the ways you, as an actor, can learn to distinguish between one way of doing something and another, the greater your ability to express something will be, the more nuanced your performance and the more sensitive you will become to how something is working. In a sense this is obvious, but it does depend on your ability to feel and make fine differences to what you are doing. Every Feldenkrais lesson is about this, and it is one of the best reasons for working with the Method.

Any actor would agree that it is not so much what you do as *how* you do it. The devil is in the detail, always. Feldenkrais often said he didn't teach people to do new things as much as teach them to do the thing they *already* know in another way – and for an actor that is so important: to be able to do ordinary actions in many ways to suit the character and the moment; to be truly responsive to the situation, the other actors, the current moment of play. And that means increasing your ability to feel, to sense, to notice differences, and so to play with differences. It may seem a bit of a jump from sensing the movement of your shoulderblade to responding to another actor, but in the end it's all part of the same thing. In the Feldenkrais Method we go back to something much simpler: can you feel what you do? Can you feel the difference between doing it like this or like that or some other way? Can you make a choice about what you do? Are you stuck with one idea about yourself simply because you haven't experienced any other?

Turning

It's best if a few people do this, so you have an audience and also so that you can watch other people try it. That way you can see the differences in how different people do it. However, you can do it on your own too.

- Stand with your back to the 'audience'. All you are going to do each time is turn to look at an imagined person coming into the room (as if from the audience). Each time you know who it is before you turn. You have been waiting for them. Don't make a 'clever' choice. Just do what comes naturally. It's very simple. Just notice what you do physically each time, and/or the audience can tell you.

- The first time you turn because someone walks in who you are madly in love with.

- The second time it is someone you don't care about.

- The third time it is someone you are terrified of.

- The fourth time it is someone you are very angry with.

Was it different each time? In what way was it different physically? How much of you turned each time? All of you? Just your head? What parts of your back moved? Did your shoulders turn? Your eyes? What was the speed? What was the level of tension in different parts of you?

The interesting thing about this game is not just that it is different each time but that, if you do it with a number of people and if you are a good enough observer, you will see that the choices they make are not, in fact, just acting choices. They are also about the ways they can and can't turn. The places in their neck, back, ribs and pelvis that are available for the movement and the places that aren't. A restriction somewhere reduces the options they have to play with and will colour what they do. It's likely they won't notice this is the case because they won't necessarily feel it as a lack. If you don't know that something is possible, it is hard to miss it. It is hard even to imagine it. It is more obvious that a piano player with stiff fingers or rigid arms will have less expressiveness, but it is also true for an actor in terms of how they are able to use their whole self. There is a lesson at the end of this section called *Sitting and Turning*. When you have done it, come back to this game and see if you make some new choices and have greater, easier or more subtle possibilities of expression as a result.

But first it is worth clarifying this aspect of learning further as it also explains something about available acting choices.

The Self-image

We could say that the sense you have of yourself is a bit like a map. But a funny kind of map where some of the parts are drawn in very accurately, some are not very accurate, while some bits are partially or completely missing. If you had to drive from London to the Edinburgh Festival with a map like that you might have trouble. Maybe you would get there eventually but it might be in a rather roundabout way, travelling through places you really didn't need to go, using a lot more time and energy, or maybe you just wouldn't be able to get there and have to settle for Glasgow instead – which is a great place to be, but not where your show is on. Or maybe your map doesn't even have Edinburgh on it, so the whole idea of going there seems impossible and a bit of mystery. That's the kind of map you may well have of yourself, which is why you couldn't feel every detail in that first lesson. As time goes on, the more attention you pay, the more you will be able to fill in the blank spaces in your map and re-route the bits that just aren't accurate or useful.

This is one, rather simplistic way of describing what Feldenkrais called 'the self-image'. These maps are not imaginary: they are a way of describing how the body is mapped in the brain, which has been much better understood with the advent of MRI and the other advancements in neuroscience.[27] Imagine, for example, that you have three or four vertebrae in your back that have gradually stopped moving separately and, over time, have started to move together as a chunk (very common). Gradually your system will have also started to sense these vertebrae not as three or four but as one, and they will be mapped in the sensory cortex of the brain like that. Very hard, then, to learn to move them separately again, until you can find a way for the brain to perceive them as separate. There was even a (rather horrible) experiment done with monkeys where they sewed two fingers together and saw what happened in the brain. The brain started to map them as one finger not two.[28]

You can probably imagine that if three or four vertebrae of the spine are sensed as one, it will limit the ways you can turn in the previous game, and that has an effect on what is available to you to express yourself. One of the ways the lesson at the end of this part will work is to clarify, distinguish parts and fill in pieces of the map so that more becomes available.

Missing Bits of the Map

You need a partner for this one. One of you, lie on your front and bend one knee so the knee rests on the floor but the foot is in the air. Without looking, make the sole of your foot flat so it is parallel to the ceiling or so that you could rest a book on it. Now, still without looking, try to tilt the outside edge of the foot up and the inside edge of the foot down. Make it a very simple movement of only tilting without dipping the toes or pointing them higher. Then tilt the inside edge up instead. The other person can tell you if you are achieving anything like the instruction. Very likely you aren't because it is really difficult to have the image of your foot and this movement clearly enough with only your kinaesthetic sense to help you. Watch your friend and see what they do with this movement too. Maybe you can film each other so you can really see what you do.

Then sit on a chair with your feet on the floor and tilt one foot so the outside edge lifts, and then the inside. Make it a very simple tilting. Nothing else. This time you have your eyes and the floor to help you know what you are doing and it is probably a lot easier. When you can do this well enough, go back to the first version lying on your front with your foot in the air – it will probably already be a bit better. Why? Because doing it the easier way, you have filled in some of your image of the foot and its possible movements, and then transferred it.

Put your hand out flat in front of you and close your eyes. Tilt your hand so one edge lifts and the other lowers, and then the other way. That's usually very easy even with your eyes closed. You have a much more detailed sense of your hand than you do of your foot – for obvious reasons. You use it a lot in many detailed ways and often without looking. Interestingly, if you ask someone to notice where their hand is they don't tend to look at it (although they might think it was a very odd question). If you ask them how their feet are positioned, they almost always look down at them to find out.

If you don't have a friend to do the foot thing with, put a book on it. A nice, thin, slippy book. It's a bit easier to feel what your foot is doing because the contact gives you some feedback, but then challenge yourself to roll from your back to your front without the book falling off. This is pretty difficult and involves more than knowing where your foot is, but that's a significant part of it...

Feldenkrais included in his idea of the self-image not just our ability to feel the relationship of all the parts of our physical selves and those changing relationships in space and time, but also our emotions, thoughts and beliefs about ourselves and the world, which together form an integrated and interlocking whole. If you live in a culture that believes moving the pelvis is unseemly, it is likely that your 'map' of the pelvis and what is involved in moving it is not clearly represented. Finding how it can move in all its ways will involve being able to feel and connect to that area, which will mean some kind of journey to get beyond those beliefs in order to feel 'allowed' to do that. As Michael Merzenich, pioneer researcher in neuroplasticity says: 'The feelings and thoughts about movement are inseparable from the movement itself.'[29]

The same can happen after an operation, attack or injury, because a traumatic experience like that can go on being associated with a certain area or movement of that area, even if the tissues have long since healed. It may have lost the definition of its representation in the brain through disuse, as it is repeated use that maintains the maps – neurons that fire together, wire together, but the opposite is also true: neurons that stop firing lose their wiring. Part of the job will be to reconnect with the area without the associated pain or trauma – to rewrite the map.

Sometimes there is a complex set of beliefs governing how the person sees themselves in the world that can disrupt the map and make it difficult to effect change. For example, one actor came to see me with a very serious pronation of his ankle/foot (a tilting or even collapsing inwards, which flattens the arch). It was so serious there was a possibility of tearing the tendon on the other side of the ankle that was being stretched by the pronation, and so an operation he didn't want was being recommended. He had a particular kind of walk – a side-bending, cowboy kind of walk, which I showed him was part of that pattern of pronation that was putting stress on his ankle. He also noticed that when we found a pattern of walking that involved more twisting – one hip forward, one shoulder back – instead of so much bending to the side, his weight shifted away from the inside edge of his heel, which undid the pronation a little and helped reduce the strain on the tendon. However, a week later he came back and said to me that this style of walking just 'wasn't him'. Something in him was very attached to his cowboy walk despite the problems it was exacerbating. Of course, I understood – and actually it had been my plan to shift him only just enough in that direction (and gradually enough) for it to be acceptable to his system, not to ask him to change wholesale in a week. Since he was both a clever person and an actor I had thought to show him where we were going because I knew it would interest him, and that the idea of a new possibility like that might engage him as an actor as well as be useful for the health of his ankle. What he was really saying was that his self-image could not expand quickly enough to include such a different style of being. Ultimately, it is often possible to expand your self-image enough over time to integrate very different possibilities. Sometimes it is a quick thing, sometimes slow, depending on how old and deep the pattern is, how key that pattern is to your fundamental sense of self, and how welcome or threatening the new possibility is.

Some actors clearly have a very limited self-image yet make a huge success within those boundaries. They may not have an incentive to 'grow' it or may have a fear of 'diluting' something that works and sells – or change may just not be welcome in deeper ways. But it's important to know that we are not talking about something that changes you or makes you less *you*. On the contrary, we are talking about fleshing out – fully mapping – what is there to be all the more you: the ability to envisage using yourself so that you can play in a myriad of ways and not be stuck in the same old, same old which limits you as an actor. And, eventually, even an adoring public can tire of seeing these limits and start to think of you as a parody of your earlier, fresher – or possibly more adaptable – self. If your map is limited, it will be hard to even contain the idea that you could walk or move in certain ways: filling in the map grows your imagination. By extension, as an actor, when you know that the way a person sees themselves, thinks and responds to the world has something to do with their movement map, you have another way to explore a character's possibilities and limitations – but only to the extent that you are not simply stuck in your own, of course.

> The only way to deal with a surprise that can come (from) any direction is to walk with substantial variability. The same with thought. The same with your operations in general... The richer, the more varied the possibilities of your movement landscapes, the more powerful you are. And the more imaginative you are and the more fun you are having.
>
> *Dr Michael Merzenich*[30]

A Feldenkrais lesson creates the conditions in which you can experience how you are and new ways you can be. It helps to fill in, clarify and redraw the maps. I had a one-to-one, hands-on session (*Functional Integration*, see Part 6) with an ex-martial artist (black belt) from a tough background. I had enabled him to find a soft and easy movement of reaching that extended right through his back without the habitual tension he carried in his chest and arms. He said to me, over and over, 'I have never felt myself move like this before, I have *never experienced myself* like this before.' The italics are the really important words to me. I hear them often from clients and students, because, as one client said to me only today, 'It's weird that you can't feel something until you have felt it.' Or we could say you cannot imagine what you have never experienced. It's not much use someone telling you to be grounded if you don't know what grounded feels like because you have no idea what you are looking for. Someone has to help to create the conditions in which you can experience that and then it's yours to find and re-find. It becomes part of your map. This man could not find how to 'be soft' even though he very much wanted to, because he had lost the sense of what that feels like. No one could tell that young actress in Part 1 to 'stand tall' or 'be strong' because she had no recent enough experience of it – and so nowhere to go with direction like that. Sometimes it takes many experiences in different ways for the new way of being to become familiar enough or unthreatening enough to be integrated into the map. For my ex-marital artist, it was something he had lost from his image of himself as a child having to deal with tough situations, and he had sorely missed it. His beginning to re-find it, in a Feldenkrais lesson that created the conditions in which he could do that, was a profoundly moving moment. In contrast, it is a great moment when my young male student actors stand up at the end of a lesson and feel themselves taller, broader, more grounded, more powerful and strut round the room, crowing in delight. Especially those for whom that is a new experience. And the young actresses who start to slough off the round-shouldered shyness of their teenage years and stand upright and open-chested. No one could have told them to do that or be like that, but now they have had that experience they have some sense of what they are looking for, of what they can feel again.

Two of the key things that go on in a Feldenkrais lesson that enable you to expand your possibilities as a person and an actor are feeling and experiencing differences and expanding the self-image.

> Each one of us speaks, moves, thinks and feels in a different way, each according to the image of himself that he has built up over the years. In order to change our mode of action we must change the image of ourselves that we carry within us. What is involved here... is a change in the dynamics of our reactions, and not the mere replacing of one action by another.
>
> *Moshe Feldenkrais*[31]

Two Principles of Learning

1. Getting It Wrong: The 'No-Rule' Rule

A big piece of learning – or maybe relearning – is learning *how* to learn. Real learning, the kind of learning that that baby was doing on the mat, involves a lot of experimentation, trial and error. Error in lots of different ways. Error that may not turn out to be error as much as just a road to somewhere else.

We are all very used to 'exercises' in which you have to do something correctly in a prescribed way to get the benefit. If you are seeking to strengthen or stretch a muscle or muscle group then it is really important you do the exercise exactly as pre-scribed, engaging the desired muscle(s) in the right way to achieve the desired effect. If you have done choreographed dance or a martial art, you will also be used to having to learn a movement or sequence of movements very exactly and that there is a correct way to do it – and many incorrect ways! But what we are doing in the Feldenkrais Method is different. We are not doing exercises, resistance training, or even actually stretching, and we are not learning a particular set of specific movements: we are learning something about ourselves, experiencing differences, expanding our self-image and discovering how we can use all the parts of ourselves together in many different ways – according to what works for what we want to do in that moment.

That baby in Part 1a didn't have a goal of hitting the toy: he didn't even know the goal existed as he'd never experienced it before. But once he did something he recognised was useful and interesting, he started to organise himself bit by bit to do it again. And again. Better and better. Many trials, much error, until the pathway became clearer, the irrelevant efforts fell away and it became simpler, easier and more effective. So in the Feldenkrais Method you explore, in a structured way, what is involved for you (the whole of you!) in a movement or small sequence of movements. You try out a variety of possibilities to feel more of what can be involved, and you improve at the rate available to you, rather than forcing yourself to do something whatever the cost. This process of allowing yourself to learn turns out to be more important than forcing yourself to achieve a specified end – which, in this context, is paradoxically more likely to take your further away from achieving anything other than strain. As Lecoq says, discussing the use of the neutral mask, 'Telling the students how to do it would be to hinder them... they would be too worried about doing it right, whereas their primary need is to experience.'[32]

So with Feldenkrais, when people first start, of course they want to know if they are 'getting it right' and are keen to know what is 'correct'. But that misses the point; in fact, there is almost never such a thing as universally 'correct'. While some ways of doing something may well work better than others, and sometimes what works for something specific is, of course, specific, most people want to extend what they have found is valuable in one situation to *all* situations – and often they are taught that way too. But, actually, we need lots of ways of doing the same thing usefully according to the circumstances. How you reach for something is going to be different depending on what you are reaching for, where it is, how far away it is, how urgently you need to get it, whether you have to pay attention to something else at the same time, how safe or dangerous the situation is, whether it is pouring with rain... and so on. Just as turning was different every time the circumstances changed in that very simple game on p. 51. Standing with your feet under the hip joints may be good practice (if you can do it) in some situations but not, for instance, if you are preparing to receive a serve in tennis or swing a golf club. Standing with your feet in parallel may be required for some activities but it is a specific demand on the ankles, hips and back that means it is not the most natural way of standing for most people, or in any way universally 'correct'.

On a different note, if someone has the experience of themselves with a very wide-open chest at the end of a Feldenkrais or some other kind of movement lesson, and that feels wonderful, it still may not mean they should be like that in everything they do. How can you wrap your arms round someone with such an open chest? How can you put on your shoes? How do you play a down-trodden woman with no sense of self-worth like that? Or a boy who is being bullied at school, unless this is his defence (could be interesting actually...)? A wide-open chest is a wonderful option to have, and it is very limiting not to have that option, but that is all it is: one option amongst many. We want many. Our choices need to be specific to the particular activity or situation. So don't fall into the trap of 'one rule fits all'.

In addition – ironically – if you constrain yourself to trying to do what you think is 'correct' all the time, you give yourself less opportunity to stumble across something that works better – just as trying to 'get it right' in rehearsal often cuts off avenues of exploration that lead to great discoveries. Todd Hargrove quotes the interview with Merzenich saying it is better 'to move to a point in space in 100 different speeds in 100 different ways... than to move 200 times in the same way to get to that point in space.'[33] Be like that baby. Allow yourself to play, to make many mistakes, to feel all of it, to discover and not to censor. The discoveries you make for yourself even when they are less than helpful will be of much more use than a list of rules, because the discoveries will have variability, context and connections. Allowing yourself to play will help you develop more of that habit in rehearsal and performance too. The idea of play and not being constrained by what is 'proper' or 'correct' is stressed by teachers as widely different as Philippe Gaulier and Sanford Meisner. Back as far as Copeau, actors have been advised to watch children play, to recapture that sense of themselves.

It's also worth asking how often you play a character who gets it 'right'? You could spend ages learning to stand 'correctly' according to some set of rules and hardly ever be able to use it because you will be playing a human being and human beings don't tend to do things correctly – especially not characters in dramas, because then where would the drama be? Rules don't help actors a lot as they will always have to break them. In Feldenkrais there are no rules as such, rather relationships and patterns, because if you can gain a sense of how all the different parts of you move in relation to each other in many different ways then that is something you never have to throw away.

Ultimately, the most important aspect, perhaps, is that an actor needs to be able to draw a performance out of themselves, so that they remain internally connected. Directors mostly seek to create situations to enable an actor to do that (in relation to the text), rather than decide what they want from the actor and give them a line-reading, because they know that imposing from the outside does not often produce a good result. Feldenkrais is useful for actors as a process because it does not impose from the outside; it too creates a situation through the instructions in a lesson and asks the actor to draw responses to those instructions out of themselves. It fosters a 'connectedness' and does not give line-readings.

John Heilpern in his book on *The Conference of Birds* says Peter Brook liked working with Moshe Feldenkrais specifically because he felt Moshe didn't work to a 'system' as such (Peter Brook did not like his actors to be constrained by methods). An important tenet for a Feldenkrais teacher is 'give the person what they need at this moment', i.e. seek to enable them to learn what they need to learn right now. That makes for some pretty different-looking lessons sometimes, especially if you are working one to one.

2. Quality Not Quantity

With traditional exercises, *more* (more weight, more reps, greater range of movement in the joint, longer, bigger, higher, further, for longer) is often seen as progress, which it may indeed be for some kinds of exercise. But when you are working to develop skill, that is not necessarily true and is, in fact, likely to get in the way. We are looking at better organised, easier, smoother, less effortful movement – i.e. *more* skill – which might mean using *less* of everything else while you are learning. More skill is likely to facilitate those other kinds of 'more' too, if that interests you. In business circles they talk about 'working smarter' rather than working harder, and the same is true here. We will return to this theme when we talk about effort in Part 3 as it is a BIG theme. This will do for now.

Lesson 2: Sitting and Turning

Stand for a moment and, without stepping, turn to look behind you. Notice which way you chose to go first. Keep going in that direction and notice the ease of the movement as well as how far you can turn and look. Don't go so far that any place feels strained, even if that limits the movement.

Listen carefully to which parts of you are involved in the movement? Do you just turn your neck and head? Are your shoulders part of this turning? How much of your back? Does it involve your pelvis? Your legs? Is the movement mostly in one place like the neck or ankles or is it shared?

Try out the other direction and notice if it goes more or less easily. What else is different about how you do it on this side?

Now sit, knees bent and with both feet to one side, so one leg is bent in front and one leg is bent behind, whichever way round is most comfortable for you. Lean on the hand on the side of the front leg and bring the other hand up in front of your face at eye level. Let the elbow hang down and let the hand flop from the wrist so you have as little work to hold up your arm as possible. Take breaks between each block of movement, but remember where your legs were so you can come back to exactly the same position.

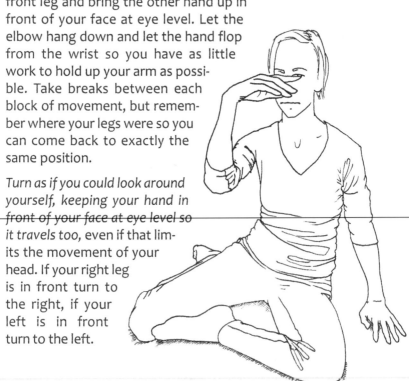

Turn as if you could look around yourself, keeping your hand in front of your face at eye level so it travels too, even if that limits the movement of your head. If your right leg is in front turn to the right, if your left is in front turn to the left.

Keep leaning on the other hand for support. When you have done this and come back to the middle a few times, turn once more as far as you can go comfortably and easily and stay there. Do not strain or force. Look beyond your hand and spot something immediately opposite on the wall that can act as a marker for how far you have turned.

Turn around again as far as you can go comfortably in this same direction. Stay there. Now turn only the eyes back in the direction you have come and then back to your hand. Nothing else – not even your head – moves. Do it many times smoothly and gently.

Test: Come back to the middle with all of yourself, close your eyes and turn again. When you have reached the furthest place you can go easily, open your eyes again and check your marker. Have you turned the same amount, further or less far?

In the rest of the lesson do this test with closed eyes at the end of each step and open them, to see whether you have turned further than your marker. Never force it. In all the following steps we will keep turning in the same direction, still leaning on the 'front' arm and still having the 'back' arm up in front of the eyes as described.

Turn once again in the same way in the same direction. Don't forget to let your elbow drop and your hand flop, but have your hand at eye level and keep it there as you turn. *Stay wherever you get to. Turn the eyes further in the direction you have been turning. Only the eyes, and back to your hand many times.* Do the test.

Turn everything again; stay where you can go easily. Move the head and eyes back In the direction you have come, but take the arm further on, in the opposite direction to your head so there is a distancing between the hand and the eyes. Then take the head and eyes to the middle and keep turning them further on, and at the same time bring the arm back in the direction you have just come so there is a kind of crossing. Make these movements many times and then *do the test.*

Turn again and this time listen to what the sit bone/buttock of the back leg does. Does it lift as you turn or not? Does it help to let it lift and lean more on the front leg as you turn? Notice how it comes back towards the floor as you return. Do this several times and then do the test.

Turn again as far as you can easily and stay there. Put both hands on the floor near the front knee or even on the other side of it, depending on how far you have turned.

Stay in that position. Move one shoulder forward and the other back and then vice versa. Feel how your back moves with this. Make this shoulder movement many times, come back and do the test.

Turn again; put both hands on the floor again near to each other wherever they get to now. Look down at the floor, allowing your whole back

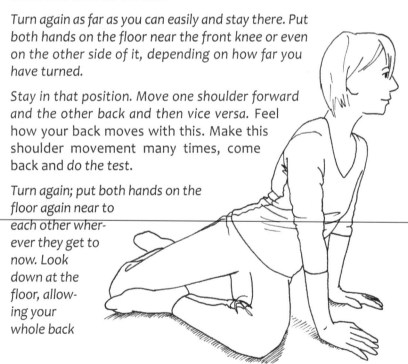

to round, and then look up, allowing your whole back to arch – but only as much as is comfortable. Let the pelvis move to help.

Do this many times and then come back and *do the test.*

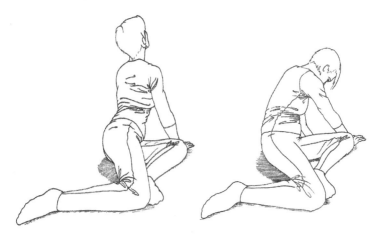

Turn again; place one hand on the floor wherever it can be and put the other on the top of your head, the elbow sticking out in the direction your ear points. Bend the whole chest so the head and elbow go down to the side only as far as it goes easily. It is tricky to define what is 'to the side' in this twisted position but make it as much like side-bending as you can, and as little like arching and rounding or twisting as you can. Swap hands and do the same to the other side.

Do the test one final time and notice how much further you turn now.

Don't do the other side yet.

Stand up, turn to look behind you in the same direction you have been turning and feel how it is. Listen to the movement carefully. Do more places join in now? Is there a different sense of ease? By playing with every part involved in turning like this, your system has learnt something that you may not have been able to put together by thinking or exercising. Several times that you did the test it may have been evident that your system had learnt something from the previous movement and just included it without you being cognitively in charge. That's kind of how it works.

Now go back and try the game *Turning*, earlier in this chapter (p. 51). Do you have more nuance available to you? Doing the game before and after with a friend can be helpful as they may see the difference even if you aren't sure. Try turning to the other side. It may have learnt something too and also be improved, or it may feel considerably less easy – and less articulate – by comparison.

Now you can do the lesson on the other side if you choose!

Part 2

Presence and Posture

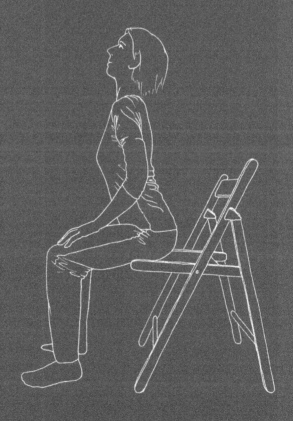

2a. Being Present and Ready to Play

Are you listening to me? Are you really listening to
me?... You're not pretending that you're listening.
You're really listening. Would you say so?... that's the
reality of doing.

Sanford Meisner[34]

So far we have looked at how the Feldenkrais Method enables
you to expand your experience of yourself and develop your
range by enabling you to feel what you are doing, explore and
discover different possibilities. We started to talk a little about
the playful nature of exploring and learning in the Feldenkrais
Method and how that is related to the ability to play as an actor.
So now I would like to delve a little deeper into a very fundamental aspect of the Method that enables the actor not just to
learn but to be ready to play – fully engaged, curious and present in the moment.

Being in the Moment

When you were doing the lesson at the end of the first part, you
were invited to feel what was happening at that moment and to
notice the movement as you made it. You didn't put your

headphones on and zone out while 'doing the exercise' (I hope!). You had to be present, tuned in and listening. I also asked you to feel what was going on *as* you moved, not just get from point A to point B or achieve a particular position. I invited you to pay attention to what you were doing as you did it and to the subtle variations; to remain 'present' and 'in the moment' all the time, i.e. to actually really do it and engage in doing it. It's not always such an easy thing to do without the mind wandering, but it is essential for learning and is actually what you have to do as an actor. Half the job is to stay present, 'engaged' in and curious about what is going on all of the time so you have a sense of the possibilities available to you. In life, people often develop an increasingly limited range of movement possibilities, not necessarily because of lack of flexibility but because we tend to stick to well-trodden pathways, and others just fall into disuse. Habits. In a Feldenkrais lesson, people sometimes have an idea of how a specific movement goes at the start, and so they just do that one thing in an automatic way without really engaging in what it is they are doing, and there is no space for a real, fresh, spontaneous – and possibly different – kind of response. Maybe that's the only way they can imagine doing it or maybe they just replay something they did the last time they did this lesson three months ago, six months before or a year before that, in a kind of 'yes I know, you say lift the arm, I do it like this and it feels like that' kind of way; or maybe they have an idea of what they think is 'correct.' But the lesson actually asks them to leave aside their assumptions, get curious about what is involved, as if they have never done it before, and so find something new in it. At the very least the quality of engagement in the movement and the sense of spontaneity becomes very different. In fact, Feldenkrais sometimes offers very novel variations of movements in strange positions, so that it's very difficult *not* to pay attention.

The same thing happens on set and onstage. An actor can be so busy enacting something according to what they did last time, or some notion of how the character should be, that they are not engaged in what is actually happening *now* – this moment. It makes the difference between the audience being really interested in watching what is going to happen next and the audience getting bored because nothing seems to be going on. Every time we embark on the journey of a Feldenkrais lesson, we practise the same kind of engagement and curiosity that is needed for acting. Something is going to happen: we don't know what or certainly we don't know how. We may have had experiences of it before, but this is *now*. We rediscover it anew every single time by simply engaging in what is happening in the moment: not repeating, 'phoning it in', switching off, zoning out or insisting on what we think is correct or is a 'good idea'. We really do it, as Meisner says in the quote at the start of this section. And that means we have to be present with and fully engaged in what we are doing, open to possibilities – whether making a simple movement in a Feldenkrais lesson or playing King Lear.

Listening In

Stand and turn your head to look to the left and right. Just where it goes really easily.

Did you actually listen to what you were doing when you turned your head? It maybe that if you listen carefully enough you will notice that it turns more easily in one direction than the other, or that you find your eyeline travelling differently – maybe higher on one side and lower on the other – if you don't interfere with it. Turn your head again and see if it is possible to notice any difference in how you turn your head to the left and the right. Already you are probably engaging in the movement differently. You are listening to what you are doing. That may mean your movement already has a different quality.

Keep turning your head gently and slowly only where it rolls easily, but change one thing each time:

- Focus your eyes as if on a ship on the horizon far away. Watch it travel slowly cross the horizon as far to the left as comfortable, and then as far to the right. Notice what it does to how you turn your head and how it feels.

- Now focus your eyes very close as if there is a small creature that is travelling from close to one shoulder, around your face, a smallish distance from the end of your nose and ending up close to the other shoulder. What does it do to the movement of your head? How does it feel?

- Now keep your eyes on a spot in front of you and turn your head – but not your eyes. They stay fixed on the spot. What happens to how you can turn your head? What does it feel like?

- Is it possible to turn your head one way and have your eyes look the other way?

- Clamp your jaw really tight shut and turn your head left and right without letting your jaw loosen at all. What happens? How does it feel?

- Have your attention on the journey of the tip of your nose as you turn your head insead (just your attention, not your eyes!), and now on your ears, and now on the back of your head. Notice the differences.

It probably feels different each time, doesn't it? And it probably subtly changes the quality of the movement. It may even suggest a different emotional situation.

And if you just roll your head simply again at the end, it may roll more easily...

In this game, just by being present and aware of what is actually happening, you become alive to the rich possibilities of subtle differences and variation available to you in what is essentially a very simple movement. This won't be the case if you are in automatic mode or just not able to fully listen to yourself. It is a kind of awareness that connects you to yourself and to the present moment in a way that not only enables you to learn, but has a relation to what you need to do when you act. You are not deciding what to do and doing it; you are discovering possibilities by listening to what is happening at the time.

Awareness, Self-consciousness and Embodiment

An acting student once brought up Meisner in a Feldenkrais lesson – and Meisner's technique of taking your attention *away* from yourself rather than focusing on yourself – and asked if that didn't contradict this use of awareness. But, to me, Meisner is actually saying something very similar in a different way. He is giving you a practical task like repetition in order to stop you consciously thinking and get you to do something fully and respond in the moment. Similar. He is advising against a sort of self-conscious thinking that pulls you out of yourself and out of the moment. Similar. He wants you to really *do* something as opposed to pretend to do it or act out an idea about how a character would do it. Same. The opposite of Meisner's reality of doing is a kind of separation from yourself by conscious thinking which I would describe as not being connected to, and present with, your whole self in the moment, i.e. *not* aware.

Moshe Feldenkrais said, 'If the person, while he is listening, while he is thinking and looking, is judging at the same time saying, "This is good, this is not good. That's it. That's not it"... at this precise moment he interrupts the ability of his awareness to see clearly and correctly.' Feldenkrais went on to describe a child, like the baby perhaps, experiencing something and being totally absorbed in it without judging or comparing:

> It is impossible to divert his attention: he just looks
> and sees what he sees. And that attracts his whole
> attention. It is the ability to observe while he is
> listening to himself. He does not have any other

attention. All his awareness is drowned in it... that childish virtue is namely the ability to look at something without preparing the fixed mechanical feedback, but instead to illuminate what is found, to light it up in our awareness, to... be nourished and sated by it without any prior deliberation and judgement.[35]

Feldenkrais is describing something very like that full engagement in the present I am proposing. It is also like Meisner's recipe for full absorption that doesn't leave space for worrying about being interesting or the character: 'I begin with the premise that if I repeat what I hear you saying, my head is not working, I'm listening, and there is an absolute elimination of the brain.'[36]

Another term we could use here is 'embodiment'. If you are not already familiar with this term it could sound nuts. Of course we are embodied. It just means 'in your body', and clearly if we weren't in some way in our bodies we would be dead. However, as a member of the audience, you appreciate that an actor who seems comfortable and 'alive' on stage often seems 'comfortable in their skin' – a phrase we all know – and you can easily spot an actor who isn't. Even in life you will be able to differentiate between people who really seem to live in their bodies and those who seem in some way uncomfortable or simply not present in theirs: stuck in their heads or sort of 'elsewhere'. But there are many levels between these extremes that include most of us in some way. It comes back to having a kinaesthetic sense of ourselves, the sixth sense that I discussed in Part 1, whereby we feel a connection to what we do, so that in any moment we are fully, physically present: alive on stage, not 'dead'. It is awareness that roots you in yourself rather than separates you from yourself.

Shifting Attention

As you are reading your attention is on the lines of the book. Keep reading but shift your attention to:

- Your pelvis/sit bones on the chair and whether you are on the back or front of it/them.

- Your breath as it flows in and out, and the places that move as you breathe: your ribs, belly, back.

- How your feet are resting on the floor?

- What you can hear elsewhere in the house or outside the window?

You can listen to many things inside and outside of you while you read. All of these things are part of being present while you are busy doing something. It's not so important when you are reading, but it is very important when you are playing a sport, fighting, dancing, singing, acting, etc....

Practising listening to yourself while doing something (like that child Feldenkrais describes), not only enables you to learn, but creates a different kind of relationship to yourself in life and on stage. In a Feldenkrais lesson we foreground and focus awareness for learning. In acting or in life, it operates more as a constant background. I remember my own first experiences of Moshe Feldenkrais's work through the teaching of his colleague Monika Pagneux. I could only describe it afterwards as the sense of having been plugged in. I could feel myself and my connection to everyone and everything else in a totally new and vibrant way. There was less in the way of myself. A new possibility for freedom of action and spontaneity that carried over into my life and my work.

Awareness

It is no contradiction to say that you need awareness on stage, that sense of being plugged in – but not self-consciousness, not those nagging thoughts and judgements about what you are doing. You can see the difference very clearly in the martial arts. In a much revered ancient Chinese 'bible' of martial arts teachings called the Bubishi, there are six principles, a number of which are relevant to acting. One of them is this: 'Techniques will happen in the absence of conscious thought.' A 'technique' here means a block, punch, kick, throw, take-down, etc. You train to perfect them for hours, weeks, months and years, with a lot of careful attention to exactly how you do it in a variety of ways. It is a very precise art. But when you are doing any kind of sparring, or preparation for sparring, you cannot be acting out ideas, consciously thinking about and judging what you are doing: that slows you down! You need to be able to respond immediately. You have to, very simply, be aware of yourself, the space, the other person, and just act. You have to trust that all the training you did is there. You must be very alive to what is happening, respond in the moment and just do it: otherwise you will not respond to what is actually happening at the time in an appropriate way and you will lose a point, get hit or be taken down. In a real fight that could mean you die for real. It is very similar for an actor who also risks 'dying' on stage. It is that total absorption in doing without judgement that the child in Feldenkrais's example has. I repeat: this does include awareness of yourself and everything and everyone around you. It's just not self-consciousness.[37]

And you have to train – so when you want it it's there and when you want to move, you are moving and when you move, you are determined to move... If I want to punch I am going to do it, man, and I am going to *do* it. So that is the kind of thing you have to train yourself into... to become one with the... you think – and snap!

Bruce Lee[38]

Another principle of the Bubishi that applies to actors as well as martial artists is: 'Act in accordance with time and change' – in other words, act according to what is happening at that moment and how the situation is changing. Be aware of the flux in the dynamic between you, the other actors and the audience as it occurs – don't just act in accordance with what you think would be impressive/interesting/funny, or would show your best profile, or worked last time. Only act in response to the other person. Another good Meisner principle.[39] It's all there too in a Feldenkrais lesson. Feel what is happening *now*. Respond to that. Explore that. Don't just try and do your idea of what the movement should be. It means nothing.[40]

All this doesn't mean to say that there is no place at any point for analysis, conscious thought and discussion. There may well be plenty in your preparation for the role during rehearsals, or in learning technique too. It's just that once you are up there performing or in the throes of improvising or trying something out, you can't be thinking in that way. I remember having a session with a student who was struggling with her character in a scene. She had tried many techniques and paid good attention to a lot of aspects of her role: going through everything the character said or everything said about them in the play; noting the given circumstances of the scene; actioning the scene; being a weasel; being mercury; finding the psychological gesture – all sorts. All had thrown up good and useful discoveries in different ways. But what she wasn't doing when she came to do the scene, was letting go of that work and just being there and responding in the moment. She was busy with all the ideas she now had about the part, and it was getting in the way. I ended up only allowing her one line of text and then provoking her and pushing her around (literally, because in the scene this is what was happening to her subtextually) until she could no longer ignore me and do her thing on her own, but suddenly unconsciously connected her text directly to the annoyance I was provoking in her. Now she actually responded to what I was doing and what she wanted me to change in my behaviour there and then, rather than to her idea of the character. And when she did she was very good; all her hard work was there informing it. Having technique in the end really means having had enough experiences to be aware of the possibilities so you can respond appropriately in the moment. But notice once again: that *does* involve awareness. In this situation, as long as she shut herself off from her awareness and stayed in her conscious thinking, nothing happened, but once she let herself tune in to herself and be aware of what was going on between us – once her head got out of the way – it just flowed, but it was still contextualised by all the work she had done.

It is like what George Mann said on his experiences of learning with Jacques Lecoq: 'When I try too hard, when I think too much about it, I'm not trusting that instinctual part of myself that just knows, that learnt it. My body learnt it. I need to trust that part of myself. I need to let go and stop trying to control everything.'[41]

So we are talking about awareness as a level of engagement of the whole of yourself in what is going on. An ability to listen and respond and adapt as the moment changes, rather than a self-conscious kind of brain activity that keeps you somehow outside of what is going on. And this awareness is always needed. You need it to learn, and it's absolutely what Meisner, and anyone else worth their salt, is after so that you can be present and ready to play.

Complicité: Being Present with Other Actors

Moshe Feldenkrais based a lot of his work on the idea that human beings are very good at adapting to changing circumstances. It's what, at our best, we do better than any other species and why we have been so successful. In a Feldenkrais lesson, you go back to a more fundamental level. What you are engaging in and listening to is yourself, the sense of the movement within yourself and your changing relationship to the ground and the space. Being present and listening to yourself in this way is also a helpful precondition for being present with and able to listen to anyone else. A useful term popularised by Jacques Lecoq for this ability to be present with others is *'complicité'*.

Philippe Gaulier, with whom I studied in my late teens/early twenties, had a wonderful phrase for actors who couldn't be present in this way: 'You are acting in your own corridor.' It was a much-dreaded phrase. It meant you were so far away from actually acting *with* the other actors that you were not even in the same room as them. You were in the corridor outside, doing your own thing, on your own. It would shortly be followed by Philippe suggesting to his neighbour in an audible whisper that they might like to leave and go to the bar instead. Drama (or comedy) on stage doesn't usually happen as a result of two people saying or doing things totally independently of each other. The drama is in what happens *between* them in the given situation. Stanislavsky says the same thing in a different way. You do something *to* someone. To affect someone. You don't just do it in a vacuum for the sake of doing it. Meisner: 'What you do doesn't depend on you, it depends on the other fellow.'[42] But in my experience you often see an actor who has carefully 'actioned'[43] every line or phrase proceed to play the thing according to the 'actioning', without any reference to the other actor, or with any sense that he or she might need to adapt their responses to what the other actor is doing. At that moment the actor is firmly in their own corridor. It is not at all what Stanislavsky intended, and it is unlikely to be what the actor intends, but it can be what happens all too easily. *Complicité* is listening and responding to and playing with the other actor: what happens in that exciting place of possibilities between people when they are engaged with each other.

There are many fine books on this topic, but what is important to us in this book is the link between *complicité* and the awareness that I was discussing. Being present with yourself and being able to listen to what is happening in the moment, and to the changes and fine differences as they happen in movement, extends to being able to listen to changes and fine differences in what is happening between you and someone else. It will make you more sensitive to more subtle changes in their voice, their behaviour, and to have that range available with which to respond. John Wright makes the point that Feldenkrais asks you to be in *complicité* with yourself, to listen to yourself and be responsive to what you are invited to do – which in turn helps you be in *complicité* with someone else on stage. As Feldenkrais says himself in a recorded conversation with actors of Peter Brook's Centre for International Theatre Research and El Theatro Campesino in 1973:

> What does increased sensitivity mean? It means telling the difference between minor increments or decrements in minor changes. It means you become sensitive to the little lead that your partner gives you, to the change in your own voice, to your partner's voice, you become more sensitive, more differentiated, more awake.

Being Present with the Audience

Being Present with the Audience

For this you need an audience, so you need a group of three minimum, but preferably more.

One of you come on to the stage and find a place to stand and look at the audience. Do nothing more than that. Very simple. Just stand and allow yourself to shift your gaze, making eye contact with different members of the audience, but doing as little as possible for thirty seconds – or if you are feeling brave, a whole minute. Then bow and leave the stage. Notice how it feels.

The audience's job is to see how present the actor can remain: Do they disappear into themselves or push themselves on to the audience in some way? Do they look comfortable? How much do they fidget and wander? Or can they simply just be present and in contact without 'doing'?

The interesting question in the above game is: what got in the way of you or your fellow actor's ability to be simply present without doing? How comfortable were you? What parts of you did you not know what to do with? Could you breathe easily? Where was the weight on your feet? Did you want to shift or wriggle? Did your eyes fix or wander? Did your mouth tighten? Did you feel tension in some places? What did your fingers do? Did you feel a rising desire to get off stage or do something? Did you see any of that in your fellow actors?

And why is it important to notice those things?

One reason is because, if you are busy with your own discomfort on stage, it is harder for you to be present with us and so for us to watch you. When we feel your difficulty with being present, it makes us uncomfortable in turn. We might not want to be present either, and we might wish to follow Philippe Gaulier to the bar! John Wright has a lovely version of this game (which he in turn developed from an exercise used by Copeau and which I know from teaching with John), in which the audience go a step further and provide a spoken commentary of what they see going on in the person onstage. Of course, it may not actually be the person's *real* story or anything they are actually thinking, but it is what the audience is getting from their presence. But it is also interesting to do without the commentary so the actor onstage doesn't have anything from the audience to respond to. It's the total opposite of Meisner giving you an activity. It drops you right *dans la merde* ('in the shit'), as Philippe Gaulier would say.

In that way it tells us something very simply and clearly about how well we can read you and what your chances are of being able to communicate what you want to us. Monika Pagneux, Peter Brook and others talk of the actor's transparency: a simple openness to the audience that enables what is inside the actor to be seen outside. I will come back to this idea in a later chapter, but I brought it in here as a simple extension of being able to be present with yourself and so with the audience. It is important to appreciate that the difficulties that the previous game may have revealed will be part of what you do onstage or on camera that will get in the way of whatever you want to communicate to us. The inside cannot transmit to outside because there is too much interference, too much internal 'noise' for you to be really present with us and for us to hear you.

This background interference (or 'noise') is often what makes it harder for the actor to hear themselves and their fellow actors, which in turn makes it harder to be responsive to the impulse to do something that could arise from the simplicity of just being there and quietly listening to themselves, the audience and their fellow actors. They are not in contact, not in *complicité*, on their own in their own corridor, outside the real play. They have lost awareness. They are all self-consciousness. We will look at some of what causes this 'noise' in Part 3.

Remember what you saw and what you felt in *Being Present with the Audience*, and try it again after doing *Lesson 5: The Pelvic Clock* at the end of Part 2b. Because, in my experience, the difficulty of just simply being present is pretty much *always* helped by 'Awareness Through Movement' (ATM). This is the name Feldenkrais gave to the lessons he taught to groups. The sections entitled 'lessons' in the book are all classic ATM lessons (or parts of lessons), and some of the games contain little moments or particular aspects of an ATM too. In an ATM we don't have to deal with an audience, with other actors, with a situation, with a text or having to come up with an improvisation. In some ways, the pressure is off. You are not being judged, don't have to make anyone laugh, are not being scrutinised by colleagues or audience. All of this can help free you from your habitual ways of coping. You are often lying down in a lesson so all your habitual ways of keeping your balance and staying upright are not an issue either. You don't have to deal with anything except tuning in to yourself and exploring the movement you are being asked to explore. It is a deliberately safe place where it feels easier to risk letting go, be spontaneous and find something new. The only risk is not getting out of the way enough to allow yourself to become aware of your habits and learn that you really do have other possibilities. To be very present with yourself. And that can be enough of a challenge all on its own.

I hope you will now appreciate that we are talking about an awareness that involves the whole of you, not a self-conscious way of thinking led by a disembodied brain. Monika Pagneux did not like the word 'warm-up' for what an actor does to prepare. She called it a *wake-up*.[44] She was right. You have to wake up to yourself, to the situation, to the environment, to the other people on stage and in the audience. You have to wake up, feel, listen and be present.

2b. Finding Dynamic Posture

If we eliminate from standing all that is extraneous to it, such as standing manly, femininely, authoritatively, nicely, efficiently, arrogantly, proudly, or meekly and all the other cross-motivations that we cultivate in childhood and adolescence with such wholehearted conviction of doing right, there remains standing, as dictated by the structure of the body and its nervous mechanisms, a stance that is rare, but of which we are all capable.

Moshe Feldenkrais[45]

In your mind, go back to that exercise of standing in front of the audience and recall what you felt. To just be present easily and simply without 'doing' is very hard. In the last section I talked about awareness, embodiment and *complicité* in relation to this and where Feldenkrais can help you simply be present. But there is, of course, more to this picture.

Posture

When an actor simply stands in front of an audience, all their habits and patterns tell a story, as we saw in Part 1 – they are all there to be read like a book, as John Wright's 'Copeau's Game' always shows. It's often at this point (if not before) that actors start mentioning their 'posture'. And when they turn up in my studio for a one-to-one Feldenkrais lesson they often say things like: 'I know I have terrible posture. My mother always told me to sit up straight and not slouch, and then the teachers at drama school always tell/told me that I have bad posture.' And then comes a list of things to do with the structure of their spine that they have been diagnosed with or issues with their 'alignment' or 'core' that they have been told they need to correct or strengthen respectively. This is not limited to actors. It is a concern for many people, but actors (along with dancers, musicians and sportspeople) often come across it sooner because of what it means for their work.

This is a huge subject. And everyone – from medics to alternative practitioners to sports and fitness trainers – has a huge amount to say about it. This is not the place to analyse or take issue with this plethora of ideas. I am simply going to present a different way of thinking about posture that comes from the Feldenkrais Method, and is very useful, especially to those in the acting world.

Here is an example of a scenario that often plays itself out in different ways in my studio, and no doubt in many others. An actor comes in who has been told there is something wrong with his posture and that this is a problem for his breath and voice (see Part 5), for his ability to be powerful, balanced, fluid, centred, grounded, and so also for his ability to be easily present as well as convincing in certain roles. He has always had tension in his shoulders, he tells me, and sometimes he has a little discomfort in his back, but only really since he started working hard at drama school or started on a particularly physically challenging show or film. He then tells me he has too pronounced an arch in his lower back, too sunken a chest and that he carries his head too far forward. I can see that all of this is true. He then proceeds to show me how he has been trying to correct this faulty alignment by pulling in his belly, sticking out his chest, pulling his shoulders back and pulling his chin in and down. The result is that while he thinks he should be more satisfied with this 'better posture', he finds he cannot breathe properly, his throat feels constrained, he feels awkward and uncomfortable and, as soon as he is occupied with something else, he forgets to 'correct' himself and reverts to his usual 'bad posture'. Moreover, this 'good posture' is something he can only maintain when he stands still. As soon as he walks, runs or starts doing anything, the way everything is aligned in this 'good posture' is required to change, but he doesn't have the myriad instructions for how everything should stack up in every different movement, so the simple version he is trying to stick to simply falls apart. This comes back to something I said earlier about there being no rules that work for every circumstance. If you are relying on tucking in your chin to have good posture, what happens when you need to look at the sky or reach up to a high shelf? And how are you going to put your shoes on while sticking your chest forward? Go ahead and try. So if the rules of good posture are defined by a specific way of holding yourself when standing but don't apply when you are actually doing anything, then how meaningful or useful are they? And if the corrections required make the actor less comfortable, less able to be easily present and less able to do anything, what makes that way of defining or improving posture a particularly good one?

Acture

Very quickly we start to move away from the idea of posture as something static to something dynamic: something that can change and adapt to whatever you are doing. It is no longer a set of instructions for holding everything in a specific alignment, but something about enabling you to do things – about how you function. Dr Feldenkrais was not a fan of the word 'posture'. He preferred the word 'acture', because posture is not a position; it isn't separate from anything else you do: it is part of everything you do. His ways of defining good posture have nothing to do with instructions to stand with your feet X width apart and hold your head/pelvis/lower back/shoulders like this or that. For example, one of his main ways of defining good posture is that you stand (or sit) in a way that allows you to move in any direction immediately without a preliminary reorganisation. He also talks about it as the skill of 'reversibility' – being able to stop or start a movement immediately at any point and change direction at any moment.[46] What does he mean? Well, try this game...

Acture

Sit on a chair however you like. Make yourself comfortable. No, really. Don't do 'good posture'. You want to know how good your posture actually is, not assume some idea of posture that you have to work to maintain.

Stand up. How much did you have to do before you could get up? Did you have to uncross your legs, shift your feet, straighten up? Do it again if you are not sure.

Sit down and get up again several times in succession. Make it better, smoother, easier. Sit down properly each time, don't just 'kiss the chair'. Give your weight to the chair fully, but without falling or dropping into it. Then stop and stay sitting and see how you are sitting now. Probably differently. Would your mother/teacher like it better?

Now stand. How are you standing? Where is the weight on your feet, for example? Are your knees locked back? How do you carry your head? Is your weight more in one leg than the other?

Step forward. And again. Keep going forward. Stop. Go backward. Forward again straight away. Stop. Wait. Now go Left. Right. Left. Wait... wait. Right! Get a friend to give you random directions like this, with random timing if you can, and move immediately but without a scramble. Make it smoother, cleaner, easier. After a while, notice how you are standing in the pause between movements. Is it different? Do you like it better?

This idea of 'good posture' (I won't use the word 'acture' here as it has never caught on, despite its accuracy) is profound. It taps into the most fundamental purpose of 'good posture', which is survival. Being able to move in any direction immediately enables you to get out of the way of danger – or into safety: to respond and adapt. Martial artists, like Moshe Feldenkrais, know this because, if you are not ready to move, you are an easy target: if you have to make a preliminary readjustment before you can get out of the way, that could slow you down enough to finish you. But this mobility, this readiness and ability to adapt and change is not just about survival, it is about how you negotiate your way in the world. That is a very big idea. It brings us back to the notion of being able to respond in the moment, which makes this view of posture especially pertinent to performance, where there is a need to be alive, spontaneous and ready to switch direction at any time.

Finding Middle

This dynamic way of thinking about 'posture' helps us understand that it is really just a resting point between movements, a point of departure and arrival. We could call it 'Home'. Like the moment a swinging pendulum hangs in the middle before setting off to the other side, and where it will eventually settle once all the movements subsides. We, however, very rarely settle exactly in the middle. When you paid attention to how you stood in that last game, you may have noticed that you had more weight on one foot than the other. Or if you 'listened' to yourself as you sat, you probably had more weight on one side of the pelvis than the other. If you didn't, try it now. I would put good money on there being a difference between the sides. It's most unlikely that you are evenly balanced. You may not notice an imbalance because it will feel familiar and therefore 'right' to you, as Home usually does. But that does not mean you are actually in the middle. Listen carefully. If you can feel the difference, what do you do about it? You could try and do something to make yourself more balanced, but then you are back to correcting and fixing and holding yourself in place. If you think back to the pendulum, it swings the same amount to the right as it swings to the left, so middle is always middle. If you push it more to the left, it will swing more to the right. And as it runs out of steam and starts to go less to the right, it also goes less to the left. It equalises. So how about if, instead of trying to fix middle, we did the opposite and tried to find movements *away* from middle in every direction, aiming to equalise those movements? Then let's see what that does to where we settle, where we find middle, whether Home simply shifts as a result.

Lesson 3: The Pendulum

Stand and feel where the weight is on your feet: toes? Heels? Insides of your feet? Outsides? More on one leg than the other? Or just differently on one foot and the other?

Imagine you can only move all together in a line like a broomstick, not bending or twisting or anything from your feet to your head. Like an upside-down pendulum.

Lean forward from your ankles so your weight shifts into the front of your feet and your whole self moves forward in a line, your head moving through space. You can only go so far before you would fall over, or move a foot to catch yourself. Don't go that far. Stay within your possible limit but feel how far it is.

Now lean backwards. Stay all in one line. Find your easy limit.

Go forward and backward like this. See if you can do this without bending anywhere other than your ankles, so that you are all in one line and your head swings through space. You can probably go further in one direction than the other, so even them up by making the direction you can go further smaller to match the direction you can go in less.

When they are as even as you can manage, start to go a bit less in each direction, and then even less, and less until you hardly move at all, so that someone coming in couldn't see you move – though you have the sense of still moving, however minimally. Feel where you are on your feet. Is your weight in the same place or further forward or backward?

Now do the same thing leaning left and right. Explore how far you can go before you lose balance, and notice if it is more in one direction or the other. Make the bigger distance smaller to equalise, rather than force yourself to go further than you are comfortable with. Go from side to side, making the distance smaller and smaller until you settle but still have that sense of potential movement. Where is middle now?

Having gone in these four cardinal directions you can now describe a full circle that is equal in all directions. Make sure you do not go more in one direction than another. Make it smaller until it is a true circle, and then keep making it smaller until you settle. How do you stand? Where is your weight on your feet? Does anything else feel different in you?

This is a good little lesson, and it's helpful for centring, as I hope you could feel. And it illustrates the idea of where we settle and of posture as simply a place between movements. But it's not the whole story because, of course, we are much more complicated than a pendulum! We don't hold ourselves all in one line – we have many moving parts that can bend and twist and, moreover, that prefer to bend and twist more in some directions than others. Again, one answer is to go the 'correction' route and have someone put you in the middle through a set of instructions like: 'Bend your head to the left more, move your ribs over to the right, tilt your pelvis down on the right, shift it over your right foot. Well sort of, can you shift it a bit more? No not like that, okay, now a bit less – okay, well, that will do. Sort of. It's a bit better. Now hold that.'

But that's going to be a tough call again, isn't it?

Returning to the idea of going away from middle, you can explore the ways you bend and twist in many directions – and if you can learn to bend and twist in many directions instead of just the few you favour, then, just like the pendulum principle, your Home is more likely to be in the middle than if you stay stuck in your habitual patterns. When you think how many variations of 'away from middle' there are for a human being, you realise that this is potentially a *huge* job – which is why Moshe Feldenkrais developed a couple of thousand lessons (and every Feldenkrais teacher develops more of their own). Plus, given the fact that improvement is always possible, you can see how it could be a life's work – but don't worry, you can usually feel a difference even after one quite simple lesson, and significant improvement within weeks or months. If you couldn't move on, discover more and improve, life would be boring wouldn't it? Isn't that part of why people like acting – because there are always more new things to explore?

Lesson 4: Making Your Posture 'Worse'

Sit on a chair. Feel how it is. What part of your bottom do you sit on? If you stick your hands under it you will find a bony rocker on each side – your sit bones (see the drawing of the pelvis on p. 107). Do you sit in front of them, behind them or on them? Can you tell? Is your lower back rounded backwards or arched forwards a bit/a lot, or somewhere in between the two? Is your chest open or a little sunk? Where is your eyeline? Do you look up, down or on the horizon (don't correct it)? Are you comfortable or is it a lot of work to maintain whatever position you are in?

Put one hand on your belly and one hand on your chest and roll back behind your sit bones, so you sit more on the back of your pelvis. Let the rest of your back and chest and head go with it, so your hands move towards each other and you find your back rounding backwards, your chest sinking and closing in front and your head and eyes looking down towards your groin. *Yes, slouch.* That's what I am getting at. Do everything that you might think is 'wrong'. But do it as well as you can. Use the whole of your spine. Are there parts that don't join in? Don't force them to do more, make the bits that do it well do it a bit less so as to match up your whole spine that way instead. If you don't force it, it is likely to work better. No one likes being forced, and the deep parts of your nervous system that govern your habitual patterns are no exception. Do you feel your back get broader as it rounds?

Now the opposite. Roll forwards on your sit bones. Your two hands will move apart, your back will arch and your whole front will open up and get longer, and you will probably look up more. Can you find this through your whole back, not just in the lower back, which tends to do this well? Make it less in the bit that does it most and try to equalise the movement through the whole of your back. *Yes, arch!* Be 'wrong' in this direction too. Do you feel some place in your back narrowing as you arch?

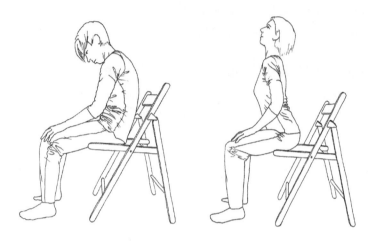

Go from one to the other gently and slowly. Do you go more in one direction than the other? Match it up. Go less in the direction you do best. Now, as in *Lesson 3: The Pendulum*, make the forward and backward rolling smaller and smaller until you can still feel the potential for the movement but no one could see it. Where are you on the sit bones? What shape does your back have? How comfortable is it? How is your posture?

So Can You Slouch Well Now? Good!

There is an inherent problem for actors in having to maintain 'correct' posture, which is that it's not that often you get to play someone with great posture. You need more variety than that. I am not legitimising all your unhelpful habits, but I am saying that you need more than a set of rules about how to stand correctly. If you need to play a character that slouches, you need to be *able* to slouch, and that means rounding your back and sitting on the back of your pelvis – which you may have trouble doing if you can only arch in your lower back. But if you need to play someone who arches their back and sticks their chest out, you need to be able to do that too – but if you can only round a lot in the upper back, you are going to have trouble sticking that chest out! That means the whole of your back needs to be able to arch and round, not just bits of it. That little lesson you have just done is great for all of that, although we only went in two directions and there are many more (see *Lesson 5: The Pelvic Clock*). Crucially, being able to go well in many directions means you will have a better 'middle' too. Marvellous. It's a nice idea that going in all the 'wrong' directions can give you better posture, isn't it? But it's true. You use these planes of movement in many ways in life and you need them *all*. None of them are 'wrong'. As Feldenkrais himself said, it's not so much a particular posture per se that is problematic for people, it is being stuck with only one option. One option, Feldenkrais would say, is like an automaton with no choice. Two options puts you at the level of a light switch. But more than two starts to make you a human being.[47] And isn't that a useful way for actors to think about it, given they clearly need as many options as possible rather than a set of rules that don't apply most of the time?

Are you worried about your voice with such 'bad' posture? The relationship between voice, breath and posture is very important (see Part 5), but while you may need to stand in a certain way to facilitate a particular voice exercise, more broadly in acting (and life), if you can only use your voice in one kind of posture, you are in trouble, my friend.

Relationships of Parts

To have good posture you don't need to fix on one specific way of having your legs, pelvis, feet, chest and head, but it is important to be clear that the way those parts relate to each other when standing isn't random either. There are more and less useful ways for them to relate *depending on what you want to do*. It is unlocking the *variety* of relationships between those parts that is going to help. In that last lesson you will have noticed that where the head is has something to do with where your pelvis is and with what is going on with the spine in between. When the pelvis moves, each vertebra throughout the spine is asked to adjust and that in turn affects the head. And so, in simple standing, if you fix where your head and your chest and your lower back should be – according to some external set of instructions which ignore how all these places actually interrelate – you are likely to be setting up all sorts of strains and efforts and difficulties. For instance, if the actor from my earlier example simply pulls in his chin rather than feeling how the length of the back of the neck needs to change, how the vertebrae at the base of the neck/very top of the back have to shift, and how the shoulders, chest, lower back and pelvis all have to respond, in turn, to make space for his head to find a new place that allows his chin to lower, then he will simply compress his throat and set up strains that he, quite sensibly, will not want to tolerate. Ironically, if he discovers how his head moves in relation to the rest of him, eventually he will also find that he is closer to the biomechanical ideal he was after in the first place: he has really learnt something about his structure and how it works. And, given he has a structure somewhat like other people's, the way he does something will start to look similar to the way other people who do it well do it too.

(Likening parts of the body to a family, Todd Hargrove quotes Tolstoy nicely in this context: 'Happy families are all alike; every unhappy family is unhappy in its own way.')[48] *But* he won't be constrained in the choices he makes. If he needs to find an organisation that is less good in order to play a particular character, it will still be available.

Being Grounded

Whenever the word posture rears its head in actor training or rehearsal, words like 'grounded' and 'centred' are never far behind. In my experience, many students and even some professional actors don't really know what those things actually mean or (more importantly) what they actually feel like, except in a rather nebulous way – and everyone can always benefit from a clearer understanding.

If you think back to *Being Present with the Audience* (p. 82), you may well have found yourself wanting to shift or fidget and been unable to simply be there, which is often described as 'ungrounded' or 'not centred'. However, it is no good simply telling an actor they need to be more grounded or more centred if they don't know how that actually feels. It is therefore best to have an experience that gives you that feeling – which is often one of the results of *Lesson 5: The Pelvic Clock* coming up shortly. But before that, it is also worth unpacking the ideas involved.

While talking about middle in relation to a pendulum swinging and where it comes to rest, I said we are not truly like a pendulum because we are made up of so many more moving parts, but there is another reason. A pendulum usually has its weight at the bottom and we have ours nearer the top. Being a sort of upside-down pendulum, a human being is top-heavy, with a high centre of gravity and a very narrow base of support in normal standing, which makes it easy for us to be set in motion in any direction using very little effort. Once the centre of gravity goes beyond the base of support you have instability or, in more positive terms, the possibility of motion, and in a human that takes very little energy. If you compare this to a four-legged animal, which has a wide base of support and a lower centre of gravity, it becomes obvious. Human beings topple into motion with the smallest deviation from middle: a four-legged creature has much further to go. We also benefit from being able to twist around our long thin axis: not so a wide-based creature. Many creatures are faster than us, but few have a human being's speed when it comes to twisting, turning and changing direction. Put yourself on all fours and feel the difference. Our upright 'posture' is all about mobility. If you think of a statue of a human being, it is not an easy thing to keep upright! One small teeter and it will topple, because not only does the statue have our high centre of gravity/narrow base of support, but, not being alive, it also lacks the self-righting reflexes we have that keep us in what Feldenkrais called a 'dynamic equilibrium'.[49] In other words, we are built not to maintain continuous stability (like a statue, which has to be weighted to make sure it remains safely upright) as much as to lose and regain stability in a continual process. This comes back to the *Acture* or *Dynamic Posture* games, which give an actor a very alive, very volatile sense of possibility rather than the life-less, static quality of a statue. But what does that mean in terms of groundedness? Does it mean we can't be grounded and have good posture? And if we naturally have a high centre of gravity, why are actors sometimes told that theirs is 'too high' and they need to 'bring it down'? Let's look at what groundedness might be and what a 'lower' centre of gravity might mean.

Being grounded is often equated with stability. Another word that is often used is 'rooted'; a sense of being welded to the ground. It brings up the image of trees and buildings with deep foundations and things that essentially don't move and are not made to move. While I have stressed that we are all about mobility, we do need stability too. If you are not stable on one leg, how can the other leg be free to swing forward when you walk?

If your torso cannot stabilise against your arm when you lift it, you will fall over. Laban contrasted 'stability and lability (or mobility)' and emphasised the need for both. The one liberates the possibility of the other. Some part needs to anchor for another to move. On a deeper level, we also need the sense of safety that comes with stability. The ability to move quickly in any direction is important for survival and safety – but safety also involves having the option not to be pushed or pulled off balance; not to be knocked over or dragged into a car; not to be pushed around in emotional as well as physical ways. Obviously this links to being able to take our space clearly and simply on stage without being pushed around by the need to resort to extraneous movement.

What do you do so as not to be dragged off or pushed around? Going back to the ideas in the previous section, you could widen your stance (think sumo wrestler), so making a bigger base of support and lowering yourself and your centre of gravity too. It both changes the way you find support from the ground and means that you are less able to topple into motion.

On stage you are not actually stopping someone from pushing you; you do want the possibility of motion and playing your role in a sumo stance might be a little strange. However, the way you find your support from the ground is key. You don't have to actually lower yourself, but you could stop doing the unnecessary work you do to hold yourself up. If you can improve this it will allow your system to become more accurate and refined in the way it finds support from the ground. You can stop actively trying to pull your centre of gravity up. 'Stopping doing' and 'doing less' are not such easy notions, I know. We are so used to the idea that we need to work harder and do something *more* rather than less. It is also not true that you do nothing to be upright, of course, otherwise you would simply collapse, but you may need a better balance between what needs to work and what needs to do less. We are actually beautifully designed so that, ideally, the weight of a person can meet the ground via a system of struts (bones) and tensile strings (soft tissue such as muscle, tendon, ligament, fascia) held under just the right amount of tension for an upright position to be maintained without conscious effort or regular strength training. This enables your bones to be maintained in a healthy relationship to each other, so that you can find accurate support from the ground up. Specifically designed anti-gravity muscles can work continuously without tiring (when did your jaw last drop open out of sheer muscle exhaustion?). If you have a sense of effort or have to work to keep yourself upright, it is a signal that your standing is not well organised and that you are, in some sense, 'falling' – muscles not designed for the job are being recruited to hold you up. In a topsy-turvy kind of way, your musculature may be working more because you are collapsing!

That can happen for a number of reasons. For example, your head can be easily maintained on the top of your spine by your structure and the anti-gravity muscles, but if it starts for some reason to fall forward, then muscles usually required for movement of neck, shoulders, etc., may have to come into play to hold it and to restrain it from falling further. These muscles are designed more for organising movement, and if required for continuous support they get tired and complain. One solution is to train or activate groups of muscles to hold the spine and bring the head back into place. If the work of the muscles that are pulling the head out of place is not undone, this approach could become a fruitless tug of war, and the person can end up held in a vice-like grip. We are back to seeking not to correct in one place as much as to re-find equilibrium through the whole. To re-find 'middle'. As I have already said: don't try to fix middle but explore different directions to enable the system to recover it.

When your weight meets the ground, the ground exerts a force on you equal to your weight (Isaac Newton's third law of motion: 'For every action there is an equal and opposite reaction'). This is known as 'ground reaction force'. It is as if the ground pushes you up. With less interference from extraneous muscular work, your weight can be better distributed and so meet the ground in such a way that you find more accurate support. This support from the ground, in turn, enables you to have a better organisation for standing: one which does not require as much extraneous muscular work... and so on. Closer to a virtuous circle. Initially, letting go of extraneous work can give you an experience of your own weight that can produce a feeling of heaviness. The sense of being pushed up from the ground through the skeleton can translate into a feeling of rootedness and yet of lightness too, especially in the upper half of the body, because inappropriate muscles are not overly tense with the work of trying to hold you up. The way we find support from the ground so that we can easily (and continuously) be held up away from it is the essence of being 'grounded'.

Conversely, once we have lost this equilibrium, the way we relate to the ground is compromised, and we can feel less well-balanced, less safe: less centred and less grounded. Often we then start to seek a sense of safety by holding ourselves more tightly and/or by holding ourselves up away from the ground, pulling up the ribs, shoulders and neck, which takes us further away from allowing our structure – and the ground forces – to do their proper job of support.

Just watch how people try to get up from a chair or the floor. Mostly they will try to pull themselves up from their head, which is nonsense really, yet many of us (most, even?) do it. The muscles of the head and neck are not powerful; they are not built to pull or drive the rest of us – only to direct. So how are we going to pull ourselves up against gravity like that? The push through the legs (aided by ground forces) and how they unfold, the righting of the pelvis over the legs and the continuing push up through the spine is what is needed to stand, and that will simply bring the head into place at the right time. Similarly, if we try to hold ourselves up from the head, neck and shoulders to keep standing, that involves a great deal of effort and strain in muscles unequal to the task. Without that work, the head and shoulders can simply rest, carried on the support of the rest of the skeleton, which is in turn supported by the ground.

Our muscle tone is turned on by our relationship to the environment. That means the very specific ways we find support from the surfaces we are on. If I am faulty in the way I find support then my musculature must in fact become engaged to support me because orientation is so crucial to me. The moment I don't have the support I will fall. What will stop me from falling? Something has to turn on to stop me from falling.

Moshe spoke clearly about how it is that we continually find support as the basis for action. He gave us the criterion that we should move in such a way we keep an even muscle tone. He gave us this criterion and he said that that happens if we counterbalance, if we find equal and opposite supports. As we become more and more specifically clear about where we get support from, the clearer we are in the muscular engagements. And it must engage. Because no living system that is healthy is going to just fall down. So the more specific, more refined, more clear you are in the way you find where you are supporting yourself from, the clearer any action you make will be.

Jeff Haller (Feldenkrais trainer)[50]

The centre of gravity varies from person to person according to ~~their weight and build, and is slightly different in women and~~ men (lower in women, as we tend to have more weight lower while men have more weight higher). It also varies with position as we have already seen (wider base, lower centre of gravity). In most people in normal standing, the calculations bring it out somewhere in the lower belly area,[51] opposite the second sacral vertebra – the traditional seat of power in martial arts. But if you are having to pull yourself up in some way you can imagine that will have an effect on your centre of gravity too.

Of course, there are many other ways and reasons we might overwork or pull ourselves up so that the support is disrupted. Sometimes a certain way of pulling the belly in can do it. Sometimes we don't allow a full out-breath, so the ribs are never really allowed to come down from the position of an in-breath, or perhaps we have a habit of holding the chest up or arching the back. We may be influenced by an exercise-based, athletic or dance training that has become ingrained, or it may stem from a way of dealing with life or presenting a certain image to the world. However it comes about, this is the sort of thing that gives people the look of a high centre of gravity and also robs them of a sense of groundedness.

Lesson 5: The Pelvic Clock

There are many ways of approaching the idea of the pelvic clock, and many variations. This is just one.

A scan in standing

- *Do you feel that there are places working to hold you up?* Sometimes it is difficult to feel because these are very habitual places that you don't notice until they stop. Do you hold your shoulders up? What places in your legs are working hard? Your belly?

- *Can you breathe all the way out or do you hold your belly in?*

- *Feel where your weight is on your feet when you are standing.* Heels? Toes? Insides? Outsides? Is it the same in both feet? Give yourself a little time with this as your weight may be shifting around a bit.

- *Does it feel like you stand more on one leg than the other?* Shift your weight more on to the leg you feel your weight in more, how is your balance there? Then the other side. How does it feel different? Do you feel balanced on either leg or is it easier on one side?

Lie on your back with legs long and scan through as in *Lesson 1: Basic Awareness*, to feel how much of you leans on the floor and where. Throughout the lesson come back to this between each block, so that you can rest a little and also notice any differences in how you lie.

Bend your knees and plant your feet. Imagine there is a clock on the back of your pelvis, with 6 down near the tailbone, 12 at the top of the back of the pelvis, close to where you might wear a belt, 3 on one side and 9 on the other. Your pelvis is the big basin-shaped structure that includes the hip bones, the wedge-shaped 'sacrum' in between the hip bones at the bottom of your spine that ends in your tailbone, the pubic bones at the front near your genitalia, and the ischia or sit bones, which are rounded bones that you sit on.

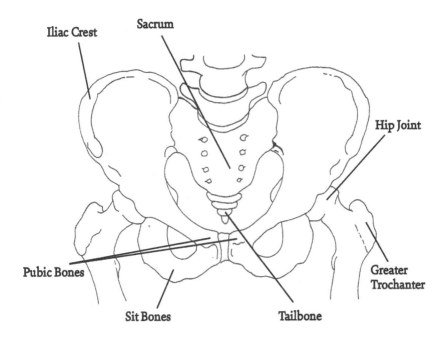

Iliac Crest

Sacrum

Hip Joint

Pubic Bones

Greater
Trochanter

Sit Bones

Tailbone

Roll the pelvis so it leans more on 6 (near tailbone) and then more on 12 (belt). Don't lift the whole pelvis ever, just tip it so one end lifts a little and the other leans. Notice how your back changes its contact with the floor as you do this too. When does the lower back come closer to the floor, and when is it pulled away? Can you allow this movement to travel all the way through your back and move your head? Soften the chest and let the movement flow through until you feel your head do something. What does it do? Does its movement echo the tilting in the pelvis?

Come back to the same movement and now listen to how you make it. How much do you work to pull in the belly to tilt the pelvis and then push the back into an arch for it to tilt the other way? Do you need to work as hard? Notice if your feet contact the floor differently as the pelvis rolls. Do you notice that in one direction the feet press a little more and in the other they are pulled at a little? See if you can emphasise pressing the ground a little to roll the pelvis one way and have a sense of the feet pulling at the ground a little (without moving) in the other direction. You may feel the tailbone – and even the whole spine pushed up away from the heels and pulled down towards them more (or just differently) by this changing relationship to the ground. You can play with these different versions. Then notice if this movement of the pelvis can travel through the whole skeleton and even nod the head so it makes its own little 12/6 movement too.

Now press the left foot a little to roll your pelvis to the right – probably 9 but depends on how you 'see' your clock. Can you find how to do that? When you connect with the ground clearly, you can transmit force through the leg bones into the pelvis, so that the left side lifts and the right side leans more. After a few movements it can become one whole integrated movement that comes up and away from your contact with the ground.

Keep doing this movement and notice where your knees go. Do they go to the right with your pelvis or stay more upright? If they go to the right can you feel how the soles of your feet tilt away from the floor too? This is not so much using your contact with the ground as using the weight of your legs to move the pelvis. It is an interesting movement too, and you can feel how it asks your whole spine to twist high up into your back.

This time, see if you can find how to do it by leaving the knees towards the ceiling and not tilting them, so you can use the contact of the whole of the left foot to enable the movement. You might feel the front of the hip joint opens up. Listen to how your belly can roll away from this leg towards the other leg – can you keep that one standing too so it doesn't fall to the right? Just let the belly roll towards it. It isn't always easy and can take time to find. Notice how this movement also travels through the whole spine to your head. Does your head move too?

Do the same on the other side: press the right foot a little and roll the pelvis to the left. Make the movement many times. Is it different this side?

Now that you have found 6, 12, 3 and 9, you can begin to fill in the hours in between. Start at 12 and then gradually find 1, 2 and 3 and come back again through 2 and 1 to 12. Feel yourself lean on these hours. How does the contact of your feet change to help roll the pelvis around these hours?

Now add in 3 to 4 to 5 to 6 and back through all those hours and 2 and 1 and 12. Find each hour carefully and then slowly join up all the hours around this side of the clock. Listen to how you use yourself to do it. Can you still breathe? Can your knees stay more or less to the ceiling? How do you use your feet? How does this movement go through your back? What happens in your head – does it do something similar to the pelvis?

Come back to 12 and find 11, 10 and 9. Take your time. Be accurate.

Add in 8, 7 and 6. Then join up this whole half of the clock, slowly and carefully. Feet... knees... how the movement flows through your back to your head.

You could then start from 12 and go to 1, 12, 11 and on from there to 3 and 9. And then from 6 to 5 and 4 and keep widening out to 3 and 9, or any other version that interests you, but listen to all the same things: feet, knees, spine, head, breath.

Finally try some full circles in each direction. Remember it is accuracy and quality of movement (smooth, easy, rather than juddery or sudden) rather than size or speed we are looking for. Can you feel how this movement involves the feet on the ground but the pelvis tilts around the top of the leg bones in response, and the movement carries on through the spine and rolls the head?

Rest for a moment with long legs and feel how you meet the floor. Do any parts of you rest differently?

Roll to the side, sit and come to standing. How do you feel? Taller? Shorter? Heavier? Lighter? Or something else? How do your feet meet the floor now? What is it like to shift your weight from one leg to the other? How well does each leg support you? How balanced do you feel?

Finding – and Keeping – a New Home

Notice what you felt at the end of that lesson after exploring so many subtle shifts of the pelvis, head and spine in relation to each other. Out of those possibilities it is likely that your neuromuscular system – the bit that does the learning and acts on it for you – already picked a slightly different 'middle' for you when you stood up. You may also have felt more 'centred' and have a sense of being heavier in some ways and maybe lighter in others too. This is what grounded feels like.

Sometimes this new way of being is immediately welcome and even a relief. I love to see those smiles of quiet delight (or even wide eyes and dropped jaws!) as people stand up and the result is revealed. I will always remember one acting student, who, finding himself able to stand easily at his full (and considerable) height at the end of a lesson, rested his arm on the top of the bookshelf, smiled down at me (I am rather small!) and said, 'Ah, the magic of Feldenkrais.' And that is not unusual. It really can be like that. Sometimes it can feel 'wrong', 'weird', off-centre, even upsetting, simply because it is new. It doesn't yet have the familiarity and security of Home. But many more experiences of this new way of being as a result of many different lessons will eventually make this and subsequent improvements feel more like Home, and you won't even have to struggle to maintain it. Partly that is because it is not dependent on one way of holding yourself. It has come about as a result of all the different parts learning how to move better in relation to each other in many different ways; whatever you do will be improved, because you are not dependent on one way of being. And partly because a movement that has been discovered, learnt and fully owned does not need your conscious attention to happen. Remember 'Techniques happen in the absence of conscious thought'[52]: you wouldn't be able to walk down the road if you had to think about it all the time! And standing is the same. Your system will simply adopt it as your new favoured habit, until you go on and develop an even better one that it decides to switch to as its new default. The theory is that your system is programmed to pick the best available option for you, but it's worth noticing that is the best *available* option. It can't pick something that isn't yet available to you. To be fair, 'best' is a tricky notion. There are strong survival mechanisms built into your system that should pick 'best', but 'best' in the circumstances can mean a number of things. Sometimes your system will revert to an older movement pattern even if it is not exactly the best, even if it might hurt you, because the pathway is that much older, more familiar and more deeply wired in, so it can be resorted to more quickly in a stressful situation. Often it reverts just because something in you (not conscious probably) still feels safer with that old familiar way even if the new way is clearly better: a case of 'better the devil you know... ' However, eventually – with varying amounts of reminders and revisiting it in lots of different ways – the new possibility can become familiar enough that your system grabs it and keeps it. The more it is used, the more deeply it becomes wired in.[53] In fact, you will probably forget or begin to doubt that it was ever really different and wonder what you were ever bothered about – until something happens to make you suddenly revert to the old way for a while or someone else points out that you look different these days or do something differently.

It may be that you are wondering what I am talking about. Perhaps you don't yet feel much difference at the end of a lesson. Keep going if you can. Some people feel big differences immediately, while for others it is more of a journey to connect to themselves and feel what is happening. It is also true that doing things from a book or a recording isn't ideal: hopefully this book will give you the impetus to find a live teacher. But even if you just begin to listen more attentively to what you do, that is a start of something that will be of enormous use to you. Because if you can't feel what you do, how can you make a choice about it?

Part 3

The Role of Tension

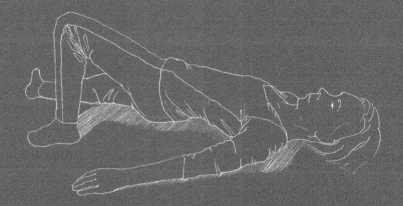

3a. Doing Less

On improvisation:

> The point is that you must start with the smallest little
> thing, start very slow and let that develop. You may not
> have a whole idea... you just follow your own little lead.
> It's precisely what you are saying: decrease intensity...
> When we come in with our own level of intensity we
> can't help but get into our habitual ways of doing
> things, but when we change that and slow ourselves
> down, then we have a greater capacity and greater
> chance of changing, of discovering new avenues.
>
> *A member of El Teatro Campesino*
> *in discussion with Moshe Feldenkrais*[54]

More Skill, Less Effort

By the end of the last chapter we were getting into the notion of
doing less, decreasing intensity and using less effort in order to
feel more, learn more, stand more easily and be present and
ready to play. So now it really is time to get in there and have a
proper look at what that means. Many actors would appreciate
the principle 'less is more' – watch Mark Rylance's performance

as Cromwell in the television adaptation of Hilary Mantel's *Wolf Hall* for a prime example of expressing a great deal by doing very little. As a universal rule it could also be somewhat constraining. In life we respond to different situations with different levels of activity, effort, urgency, ease or tension. Different characters respond differently too. Jacques Lecoq expresses something of this in his famous description of seven levels of tension in performance.[55] There are also shows and films that demand a big character, or a bold, even epic style of performance that invite the actor to 'do' a lot or to push their boundaries. So what does 'doing less' actually mean?

Playing big or epic characters and taking risks is not the same as doing *more than you need*. The amount of effort you use needs to be appropriate to the situation rather than compulsive. To shift sideways for a moment: in sport, some things *do* take a lot of effort. You can't run a marathon or even once around the block without making an effort. You can't leap or fight or lift a bag of shopping. Every time you do anything muscles have to contract, and that takes energy (or effort). It's just that there is an appropriate amount of effort for a given movement, activity or moment of performance – big or small – and that is the crucial issue. Very often we do more than we need because we are not skilful enough, because we lack clarity about what we are doing, or because we just think we need more effort than we do. Sometimes we are stuck in the idea that the greater the effort, the greater the impact or the benefit.

On the beach with my daughter and her friends recently I was dragooned into a mini-game of baseball, which I have never played before (and it's a very long time since I even played rounders). One of the parents organising the game happened to be a PE teacher and knew what they were doing. I was determined not to shame my daughter so made quite a deal of whacking the ball really, really hard. At least, I thought I did, but what actually happened is that I made a great demonstration and a huge effort to whack it and completely missed. It took several goes like this till the PE teacher took pity and said, 'Don't swing so much and stop trying to hit it so hard – just watch the ball and aim to make contact with it, that's all.' I did. It went sailing off quite a distance just on the rebound: reducing the intensity enabled me to be more accurate. The lesson for an actor: less unnecessary effort, less overt demonstration of intention, and more simple clarity of execution.

Skill is often more about inhibiting unwanted movement and being more accurate than doing more, whether you are thinking of a big gesture/action or a tiny one. Think of the little baby in Part 1. He waved his arms and did a lot of extraneous movement until he could feel how to limit the unfruitful aspects of the movement and direct his arm to reach out and knock the toy down. I am sure you can think of your own examples.

> The aim is healthy, powerful, easy and pleasurable
> exertion. The reduction of tension is necessary
> because efficient movement is effortless. Inefficiency
> is sensed as effort and prevents one doing more and
> better.
>
> *Moshe Feldenkrais*[56]

If a movement is well done it should not involve a sense of effort in the organisation of the movement itself. It should not be laden with tension that does not serve the intended action. This doesn't mean that you should not ever exert yourself or that it should feel like nothing to run a marathon. If you have to exert yourself just to put one foot in front of the other (i.e. in your basic running gait), it is an indication that your fundamental physical organisation is not good enough – you will not run as well or as fast or be able to keep going for as long as you otherwise could. It's the same with a big part in a show or a film. It may take a lot of energy, concentration and commitment, it may involve finding a larger-than-life character or require a grand or epic style of acting, but if you strain at it and do more than you need – even by a little – in a gesture or in your whole way of being, then that's all we are going to see: strain and effort. You are going to cloud your real intention and you will not communicate effectively or believably to your audience. (Unless what you want to communicate is strain and effort, of course, but then you still need to be able to choose that as an option, rather than it simply be compulsive because you can't do anything else.)

Using skill and efficiency rather than tension and effort is of great importance, so that any specific choice the actor makes will read, and is not lost in a system that is habitually strained by being at cross purposes with itself or blocked by inability. As Monika Pagneux says, 'Gesture is a silent language that writes in the space and its writing is the same as literary writing [quoted from Paul Beluge]. You must be able to read a gesture or you can't understand the story.'[57] And I would add that it is when the gesture is not clear in its intention or well-formed in its execution, or clouded with extraneous effort, that the audience can't read it. Those habitual tensions and efforts make it harder to feel what you are doing, harder to notice fine differences, harder to hear what other actors are doing and harder to make a finely nuanced response. It's that background noise again. There is even a nice psycho-physical principle to explain it which Feldenkrais talked about a great deal and which informs his Method. It's not new and there have been updated versions, but this idea was first expressed over one hundred years ago in a mathematical formula that shows how much sensitivity you lose according to the amount of 'noise' already going on. It is called the Weber Fechner Principle and it goes like this:[58]

Change in Sensitivity=K (change in I/I)
or S= Log I + Constant[59]

...which I confess means nothing me.

Sensitivity Versus Noise

What does this principle mean in 'real life' terms? If you pick up a book you can feel the weight of it on your hand via the amount of effort generated by your musculature to hold it up. But if you are holding up a piano and someone puts a book on it you won't be able to feel the extra weight of the book because of the 'noise' from the effort your muscles are already making to hold up the piano. This is a fairly extreme example, but it works for more subtle applications too. Feldenkrais said that the proportion above which you could feel a difference worked out at about an additional 1/40th of the effort you are already making, so the less background effort you are already making, the smaller the differences in levels of work you do additionally that you are able to discern. Strictly speaking, it's not a proportion of the effort itself but of the 'sensory excitation' generated by the effort: I have called it 'noise'.

> Weber Fechner: The threshold of sensitivity to sensory excitation is a certain fraction of the overall excitation already present... So you want people to move thoughtfully and gently, noticing everything, not pouring all kinds of sensory excitation into the system, then they can notice all sorts of subtle changes.
>
> *Barratt Dorko, physiotherapist*[60]

Or:

> If you keep shouting all day what change will there be? There will be a change – you will be hoarse!
>
> *Moshe Feldenkrais*[61]

For example, imagine an actress who carries considerable tension in her shoulders, chest and belly. She looks as if she never breathes out, and a director has cast her as an angry young woman because she has that look of having something held in, something brewing inside. Now the director wants to see little glimpses of that anger, not everything at once, but the actress just doesn't seem to be able to get it: she always does too much or nothing, she has no sense of what could lie in between. 'No, save it, save it for later,' the director keeps saying. 'We just want a flicker here, almost imperceptible, and then a tiny flash there, so we get the idea of what she is hiding. Then we can have more here, and then really let it go for just that bit there.' The actress thinks that's pretty much what she's doing but the director is getting frustrated because she sees no difference, just the same burst of anger. The actress can't differentiate between states well enough because there is too much background noise (sensory excitation) generated by the tension she carries all the time. She has to do at least 1/40th more than the background noise to feel what she is doing, which in her case turns out to be quite a lot. That means she just can't feel or find those kinds of subtle shifts: she can only make bigger jumps. And before you say, 'Well, that isn't me' – how do you know? This is all of us to some degree.

Or take the actor who has been employed because they want someone who can move well. He is an acrobat, damn it, of course he can move well! He is strong and powerful and skilful in many ways. He can leap and flip and do all sorts of tricks, but he does them with impetus and force. His quality of movement lacks delicacy, not because he is not flexible in his joints but because he is habituated to a level of effort that he uses in almost everything. So when it comes to taking the hand of the actress his character is meant to love, he does exactly that. He just takes it. We see no sensitivity in that gesture. 'Softer, more gently, more hesitant, more tenderness please,' asks the director. 'Look, she is soulful, she is delicate, you want to know what it is just to feel the softness of her skin.' The actor lifts his shoulders, holds his chest, screws his face up into an expression of anxiety, holds his breath and stretches out a stiff hand to grab hers in semi-slow-motion. It is a *performance* of tenderness, but it is *not* tenderness, which is a nuance not easily available to him. It is not that he doesn't get what the director is saying – he certainly isn't stupid – it's just that once again the background noise is too high for fine differentiation in the quality of his acting. I am not saying this applies to all acrobats, but I *am* saying that some degree of this lack of noticing is there in all of us.

> Clown training teaches a kind of deep listening to one's self and the audience. Feldenkrais teaches deep kinaesthetic listening. Both practices will encourage you to listen to yourself and respond gently and authentically. Try and force a funny thing in clowning and you discover very quickly how delicate humour can be. Try and force a movement in Feldenkrais and you discover how little force can actually accomplish (aside from pain, force is great for accomplishing pain!). You learn very quickly how the delicate and small make the big changes. In clowning, your biggest success might come from the way you open your eyes. In Feldenkrais, your biggest improvement might come from the same.
>
> *Emily Davis*[62]

Ways of Working Less

In a Feldenkrais lesson, the emphasis is on lowering the overall state of tonus (the base level of activity in the muscles) – or we could say lowering the intensity – so that you are able to feel more accurately what you do. This will help you to notice the difference between small movements in order to learn. And in the long run, it will enable you to develop the ability to live, behave, do – and act – with more skill, more efficiency and less effort overall, even (or especially) if what you want to do involves very energetic or demanding activity. The invitation to lower the intensity is part of the reason so many Feldenkrais lessons happen lying down, the movements are small and you are invited not to strain. As per the Dorko quote earlier: it lowers the amount of 'noise' in the system so you can 'hear' (feel) what's going on properly.

The Method enables you to learn how the whole of you works together – in synergy – to enable something to happen more easily (so, again, with less noise). You learn to spread the load of the work through the whole of you, so everything works to a purpose with a more even tone, rather than parts of your musculature working hard in isolation or even fighting other parts that are (unintentionally!) working against the intention. As Monika Pagneux says about what she learnt from Feldenkrais:

> I was fascinated: suddenly I feel the movement running through my body. Yes, I research and I work with the body for years and years... and suddenly I *feel*. It was not only in repetition of forms... it was in a deep relationship with my brain and my whole body. When you move and you lift up the arm, your whole body is engaged. The whole body... all together. It is not a part here and a part here.[63]

Lesson 6: Lifting the Head

Lie on your back on the floor. Bend your knees and plant your feet.

Lift your head a little. Feel how heavy your head feels, how easy or difficult it is, what you do to lift your head. Try and speak while lifting your head – how does it sound?

Interlace your fingers and bring your hands behind your head. Use your arms to lift your head. Easier? Probably.

Notice if you have your elbows out flat or if you bring them forward to make a hammock of your arms. Try the opposite version and see if it makes a difference. Notice that elbows out gives you a flatter back and elbows forward rounds your back a little. Which one makes it easier?

Where do you look with your eyes? Notice that looking down towards your groin as you lift your head makes you rounder and looking at the ceiling encourages you to keep a flatter back. Which helps?

Rest for a moment and just breathe. What moves when you breathe? Belly? Lower ribs? Chest? Upper chest? For a moment direct your breath so that the ribs lift and open when you breathe in and then sink and close when you breathe out. Put your hands on your breastbone/ribs and feel the movement they make. (This is not about correct breathing, this is about feeling what your chest can do.) Notice that breathing in like this lengthens and expands your front, and breathing out collapses and shortens it

Keep one hand on your chest and one behind your head. Breathe out and lift your head at the same time. Encourage the breastbone to move in the way it is going on the out-breath. Feel where your weight shifts further down your back as your head comes up. Allow yourself to listen to those shifts of weight, allowing your back to lean on and find support from the floor in each place. Do the opposite. Breathe in as you lift your head – a big breath right into your chest up to the collarbones. It's likely that your back will come up more as one piece. Go back to the out-breath as you lift the head. Which is easier?

At this point it's worth checking what you are finding. If you are used to doing sit-ups in a gym, your way of doing them may feel 'easy' just because it is familiar. However, some ways of doing sit-ups are designed to be difficult so that you work your abdominal muscles more. The ease and efficiency we are looking for here might be asking for something different, so go slowly and carefully.

Add in lifting and bringing your knees up towards your chest several times as you lift the head. Use your arms and direct your eyes in the way that makes your back rounder. Bringing your knees up makes you even rounder. Everything is going together to make your back round now: breath, eyes, synergy of the muscles in the front and back.

Try the same thing with your feet on the floor, but just rolling the pelvis up a little towards the waist (12, don't lift it, just roll it up as in Lesson 5: The Pelvic Clock).

Now leave your feet on the floor and lift your head without your arms. Did your head get lighter? Speak with your head lifted. Is that easier too?

Is it different in standing too?

In this lesson you learn how to use the whole of you in synergy to lift the head more easily. This idea is present in every Feldenkrais lesson: how do the different parts of you relate and not fight each other to enable you to do more with less strain.

But there was another aspect to lifting the head if you noticed: feeling where you lean on the ground to help support the head in the air. For something to be lifted it must have support. I talked about this in the section on being grounded. If there isn't accurate enough support through the structure from the ground, more muscles have to engage to help out. In a more general way, we lie down to sleep, sit down to rest, prop ourselves up on ledges (and bars!) to give our muscles a break. It's obvious put like that, but we are not always able to find the more specific support we need in standing and movement. Recruit the support of the ground well and your musculature can work more evenly and accurately. We come back to what is behind being grounded.

However, let's take it further. When you are clear about how you contact the ground, you can recruit that support to help transmit force through the densest material in the structure (bone) – which will push the next bone along into movement depending on the angle the bones meet at the joint. Using this principle enables you to create movement with less effort.

Lesson 7: Using the Ground

Lie on your back and bend up the right knee and plant the right foot. Left leg is long. Do something that allows you to lift the right side of the pelvis and roll to lean more on the left side of the pelvis. Don't lift the whole pelvis off the floor, just roll it to the left, leaving both shoulders on the floor.

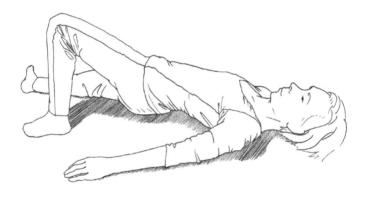

What did you do to make that happen?

1) *Using more of you and letting the movement flow through helps:*

- *How high up your back and ribs can you turn a little as well to help out?* Come and go many times, allowing the movement to travel a little higher up your back each time (without straining, keep it easy and gentle). Listen to how your ribs can gradually join in with the twisting movement – right up to your collarbone! (Both shoulders stay on the floor if possible.)

2) *Using the ground can help:*

- *What do you do to make the movement? Do you think of lifting the right side or finding support from the left?*

  Try lifting the right side and feel how much work you do.

  Now don't think of lifting the right side but think of the left side supporting you.

  Use your ribs as a ladder and think of leaning on some higher 'steps' in the ladder towards your upper chest and left shoulder each time. The right side will lift anyway if you lean on the left. What's the difference in your sense of effort?

- *How does your foot meet the ground and how do you use it?*

  Do you remember *Lesson 5: The Pelvic Clock*, where we asked where the knee was directed and which part of your foot you pressed with? Try it out and see what helps direct the movement upwards towards the top of your chest.

  Your knee could flop to the right or stay towards the ceiling. It could move a little away from your head as if someone pulls it, or stay more or less where it is. Which version allows you to connect the whole foot clearly to the ground so that you can make use of the 'ground forces' (see p. 103) to send the movement away from the floor and up into your chest?

- *How do you initiate the movement?*

  Squeeze the buttock (gluteal) muscles in the right side to lift that right side. Notice the level of work and your sense of contact with the ground. Now don't consciously squeeze the buttock. Once again, look for a clear contact with the ground, so that the movement is directed away from the floor, up through the skeleton to your upper chest and shoulder as one integrated movement. It is not that your musculature won't work – of course it will. You can find a more even distribution of work that will be more economical and enable a simpler transmission of force.

Is there work in the buttock muscles? Of course there is, but not the same as when you actively squeeze them. They will just do what they need to as an integrated part of your musculature in response to your connection with the ground. But not more. Some people overwork in their legs and gluteal (buttock) muscles, some pull their pelvis over with their back muscles, some activate their abdominals. It can be a relief to find you don't need to.

Sometimes people find it tricky to feel their contact with the ground at all, let alone how it relates to creating movement. If you are not sure, just lift the right foot a little and drop it. Let it hit the floor (if that feels okay to do). You will feel the movement ricochet through the skeleton. Now stamp a little and then find how little you need to stamp, or even push. Now think of not actively pushing. Instead simply notice how your foot connects to the ground in such a way that a force can travel upwards through you and helps your pelvis roll to the left.

Spreading and balancing the work, using your contact with the ground and transmitting force through the skeleton, as above, all help you do more by doing less, but what these lessons also do is change your image of the movement. Sometimes we just have the idea that it will be hard work, and we act that idea out. Making extra effort can be *so* ingrained you have to find a way to catch yourself doing it. Often we have anticipated it already before we even start!

Just Starting...

Go back to Lesson 6: Lifting the Head. Lie on your back. Bend your knees, interlace your fingers behind your head.

Lift your head. Remind yourself how you do it, how it feels.

Now don't *lift your head – imagine you are going to lift your head and then stop before you do.* You will feel how you prepare the movement.

What did you do to prepare? Did you tighten up and hold your breath at all? Or did you feel where your back would press the floor differently, what ribs would need to bend in the front, where your eyes would look, how you would breathe?

Go to lift your head again, but don't lift it. Instead imagine the movement. How easy is it – how effortless? Feel where in your chest you need to sink, what place will find more support from the floor or peel away from the floor, how you will breathe, soften and fold, where you will direct your eyes to make it really easy and where your elbows will go to help you round. Notice any moments where you tighten unnecessarily or hold your breath. Do you need to? Is it possible to take out of your image of the movement the idea that you need to work hard to lift your head?

Actually lift it once again and feel how it is now. Is it easier? Does it mean you don't make an effort to lift the head? No. Of course you do. But only the appropriate amount.

Less Is More

At the start of this part, I said many actors would appreciate the phrase 'less is more', but I didn't say why. We have already covered quite a bit of ground in answer to that, but there is a little more to say about what happens to the audience when an actor does less. Remember my suggestion that we are all busy reading people and situations so that we know how to think and behave? We will all do it according to our own experience and world view, we will do it rightly or wrongly or anything in between, but we will do it. It's the same kind of idea here: human beings are built to make meaning out of situations. Our brains are keen to organise and make sense of what we experience.

A well-known example is this image: **I3**
It reads one way seen like this: **I2, I3, I4, I5**
And another seen like this: **A, B, C, D**

The literature around perception and how our brain orders the world and makes meaning is vast, ranging from Merleau Ponty to John Berger and beyond, and I am not going to even dip my toe in it. It is enough to observe that we are adept at making meaning – and will do so out of whatever clues we have. Take a photo of a reasonably expressionless face and see how you read it differently depending on what pictures you put before it and after it. If you use images of sun-dappled woodland glades and flowers and a group of people having a picnic, the face will seem to be expressing a different emotion than if you use images of violence or death around it. You can get the same effect putting different music behind an image on a screen or a scene in a play. It's one of the fundamental ideas behind any montage or editing technique, from *Battleship Potemkin* through Hitchcock and onwards. In the examples I gave, the picture of the face itself does not need to show anything as the watcher will always do the work to create meaning from the context.

I remember doing an exercise with director Neil Bartlett where, one by one, we just sat in a chair, looked at the door for several minutes, then stood up slowly and went to open it. We did nothing else: thought as little as possible, acted as little as possible, kept it as simple as we could manage. Everyone watching had a story for what was going on, for, as John Wright says, meaning rushes into a vacuum. The audience does the work. The power in the actor doing less is that the audience, busy finding meaning, often sees and experiences more.

Neutral Mask

This exercise also sounds like something you might do if you work with neutral mask. Neutral mask is an excellent tool in exploring how you can let go of unnecessary effort and do less. It is a great partner to Feldenkrais work. The neutral mask was developed by Jacques Lecoq from Copeau's 'Noble Mask',[64] and is a full, plain white or leather mask with a very simple, well-defined, symmetrical face. This invites utter simplicity of movement in the wearer and is wonderful for revealing the gaps in the person's ability to answer that invitation (unlike the character masks that are sometimes very expressive and seem to demand a pronounced style of movement and behaviour).

Jacques Lecoq developed a very specific 'elemental journey' for teaching with neutral masks, which is excellent and the best known way of working with them, but they are also very useful in a number of other ways. Think of Copeau's game in which an actor stands in front of the audience with the idea of being simple and at ease, and the audience's job is to register how much difficulty the actor has just being there. In a workshop John Wright and I were teaching together, we were playing that game. A few minutes in, John slapped a neutral mask on the player and immediately the actor quietened down: they stopped twitching, they became more still, it was much easier for them to be there. With some actors, the difference was quite shocking.

The mask took the pressure off them to 'do' or to be busy with trying not to do. They could watch us from behind it. The tables were turned. They were at ease. Much of their tension dropped away. This was Copeau's discovery: he put a handkerchief on the face of a particular actress and the tension and anxiety that had been getting in her way disappeared. He then developed simple white masks which he called noble masks, because they were like the masks the nobility wore to protect them in the street.[65] The masks were not for performance but for learning a different way of being on stage.

A neutral mask cannot suddenly remove every aspect of habitual tension in an actor. It just lessens the demand on them and so changes the game. It removes the awkwardness and anxiety that are to do with performance, with being scrutinised and with being asked to do nothing, which can be considerable. Being asked to be on stage doing nothing is, after all, the very opposite of Meisner's technique of giving you a task in order that you can stop thinking about yourself. Wearing the mask has, in some ways, a similar effect.

The mask will not take away your deep, habitual patterns. In fact, it also does quite the opposite: it reveals them. As Lecoq says:

> The neutral mask puts one in touch with what belongs to everyone, and then the nuances appear all the more forcefully. These are not the nuances of character since there is no character, but all the little differences which separate one performer from another.[66]

The demand is for the actor to match the simplicity of the mask, but while the difficulties of the moment may drop away when the mask goes on, the deeper, older, more habitual tensions – twitches, particularities of stance and movement – become very loud: the attack with which a person moves, the fluidity or lack of it, where they move from, how they hold their shoulders or any of the rest of themselves, the way they walk or where middle or 'Home' (or 'neutral') is for this person, are all there to be seen.

John Wright told me that he spent a long time trying to explain to a Balinese mask-maker (and priest and performer) called Imadi Bagus Alit what a neutral mask should be like. It was a difficult job. Eventually Imadi gave the mask his own name: 'man about to do something'. For me, this is perfect. In Part 2b on posture, we said 'Home' or 'neutral' is a place from which you can go anywhere immediately without a preliminary rearrangement, and that this is a seminal idea in the Feldenkrais Method: that muscular tone can be so evenly distributed that a person can move easily in any direction at any moment (and change their mind at any moment too). And it turns out that this is a prime quality of the neutral mask as well: about to smile although not smiling, and at the same time about to swear though not swearing. The moment of evenness and readiness to go anywhere: just not gone yet. Through working with the neutral mask in many different simple tasks, the actor can find that quality of being available and ready for any story – without the story being already told.

For this they will need to be able to simplify their movement, but while the mask will point the way and enable to some degree, often more is needed – and that is where Feldenkrais is a great partner. Go back and re-read Part 2 with this in mind: for 'middle' or 'Home' read 'neutral' and you will get part of the story. Go forward and read Part 3b on power and economy, and you will get more of it. Neutral, like good posture, is not a set of rules or a constraint that is limiting, but a place people come to when they are truly in the middle and have all the possibilities of going this way or that way – in terms of colour, quality, speed and style of movement. It is when an actor can get out of their own way enough to just do the action at its simplest with the minimum of story attached – not to be a robot stripped of their unique qualities, but a living, breathing person who contains all the contrasting and varied stories they might want to tell. 'Man (or, of course, woman!) about to do something.'

Two people come to mind as examples. One a beautiful, tall, elegant actress who it was hard to fault. She didn't seem to contain excessive tension, but there was something she brought with her that I could not put my finger on but that was getting in the way and seemed to colour everything she did. When she put the mask on and turned around slowly to face us, I nearly jumped and wanted her to take it straight off. I felt like it was revealing an aspect of her which was not safe to be seen – in front of us, suddenly, was a terrifyingly vulnerable lost child. Of course I don't know how much that was really something of her or just how it was that day, but that was the story the mask revealed as it showed up lack of skeletal support, the lack of tonus and the ways she compensated. It was interesting that all this was not as immediately obvious without the mask, as she had obviously developed ways of concealing it, and yet it still underlay and quietly undermined everything.

The other, at the opposite end of the extreme, was an energetic, vibrant and quite funny actress who simply looked frenetic and anxious in the mask. All her movements were too sudden, too staccato and too small for it. What had read with a certain charm when accompanied by her jokey smile simply didn't work without. She was unable to let go and meet the invitation to find anything simpler. She hung on to her story with the mask on, and now it looked desperate. Did it matter given she had something that sort of worked without the mask? If she only ever wanted to play sudden, staccato, jokey characters in the same way, maybe, but it allowed her no room for anything different. And at some point that desperation would become visible and get in the way.

John and I followed up the initial mask experience with *The Pelvic Clock* (p. 106) and then asked our actors to stand in front of an audience again. It was easier for everyone to meet the demand of the mask, or to be in front of the audience simply and quietly without it. This lesson can enable an actor to shift their patterns enough to find a different middle, a simpler, more grounded Home, a more effectively neutral place, as you may have already discovered for yourself. But this one lesson is not enough to transform someone for ever on its own. There are very many lessons that have this kind of effect in different ways by addressing different aspects of movement. You will find a few more as the book progresses.

> I want neutrality only to free you from the inhibition of having one speciality.
>
> *Moshe Feldenkrais*[67]

3b. Power and Economy

Do less until you can do intelligently. It's only when
you can do intelligently that you can do more.

Olena Nitefor, Feldenkrais trainer,
Manchester Advanced Training, April 2015

Moshe Feldenkrais and Mikonosuke Kawaishi Sensei 7th dan Judo (Paris 1930s).
Skill more than strength.
© International Feldenkrais Federation Archive

Strength Versus Tension

We have seen that just doing more does not mean having more clarity or skill, but nor does it always mean more power either. I often find it is a sticking point with actors for whom strength and power – and, of course, fitness and body image – are often deep concerns. Young actors often want to work and train hard to achieve these ends, but, if pushing and straining becomes a habit, not only does it interfere with their acting but they may end up thinking they need to use tension and effort to appear powerful on stage or screen. As a student of a demanding form of karate myself, I am not about to downgrade training, but it's very important to understand a few things about the role of tension and what it means to be – and appear – powerful.

As everyone knows, you need to contract muscles to do anything, and that contraction involves tension. But if muscles habitually contract and tense beyond the length of time or the degree required for a specific activity, you are into the whole picture of inefficiency, as well as too much noise and reduced sensitivity. We have already seen that the latter is unhelpful for an actor, but in this chapter I would like to point out that tension on its own doesn't even make you strong. Anyone who fights well knows that, if you want to deliver a powerful punch, you have to contract and tense at the very end of the technique in order to deliver the force you have generated – but not from the start. Many people have an image that the punch will require a big effort and so everything tenses up right from the beginning, but that means they sacrifice speed as they can't move fast when everything is tense. Newton's second law of motion says that force = mass x acceleration.[68] Acceleration needs a certain softness or 'compliance'. The effort comes mostly from an initial impulse from the legs and hips that whips through the back and chest and enables the arm to be thrown out. The co-contraction (tension) comes only momentarily right at the end of a punch to deliver the impact. As biomechanist Stuart McGill, who has worked with many a power-lifter and Olympian, points out in his book *Super Stiffness*, there is a great deal in the timing. For him, a great sportsperson or fighter is the one who can go from softness (compliance) to tension (co-contraction) and back again fastest and most completely.[69] Habitually carrying excessive tension will even get in the way of generating a powerful contraction, as those muscles will be already part-contracted and so not have their full length available to generate power. Again, Feldenkrais (himself a fighter) emphasised that this did not mean being permanently relaxed.

> [It's] not just to relax! If you really relax you can't do anything! A properly relaxed person has difficulty in collecting his members to move. What we want is eutony, which doesn't mean a lack of tension, but directed and controlled tension with excessive strain eliminated. This is not flaccidity, but muscular tension only equivalent to the demands of gravity.[70]

Strength, Skill and Economy

In *Lesson 7: Using the Ground* you didn't work more, you worked better. You used your whole self in relation to the ground more skilfully, and that enabled you to hold your head up against grav-ity more easily, with more support and less unnecessary effort. Gaining skill and so increasing power may include the principles of spreading the work; recruiting the more powerful muscles; ensuring muscles that need to release (antagonists) do not tighten and work against the muscles that need to contract (agonists); coordinating eyes and breath optimally with the movement; and using the skeleton and the ground to maximum effect. But it is also about learning the ways to limit the movement in order to get the action you want, rather than doing more. In other words, limiting any random or unnecessary parts of the movement so that you improve your accuracy: economy. When power is required, it is not a wild rush in all directions, like the baby who has not yet learnt to knock the toy over; it is a controlled, focused, directed use of everything to a specific end with all the extraneous movement pruned away. A powerful movement like a karate punch or a judo throw requires good use of the whole self, transmission of force through the skeleton, but also a very precise economy of movement to execute a very clear intention. I think of Sensei Linda Marchant 7th dan (with whom I have often had the honour of training), launching herself from the back foot to knock an attack out of the way and take a person's throat in a split second of clean, focused skill and speed. She demonstrates immaculate use of self and the ground, great precision, economy and clarity – and enormous power.

It's unlikely that you would be asked to act with that kind of force on stage (although it is actually a beautiful thing to watch), and even on screen it would only be in action sequences and then it would include an element of illusion (or the business would lose rather a lot of actors and stunt doubles!). More widely, though, what we sense on stage or screen as powerful is the potential power which lies in the directedness, the control, the clarity of intention and indeed the economy that an actor has in their whole way of being. These qualities can make us believe that they can harness their whole self and every bit of energy to do what they want at any moment – whether that is to take action themselves (even if we never see it), to direct others, or simply to command attention. Idris Elba as Stringer Bell in *The Wire* is a classic example of this. Yes, we can see he is a big, muscular man – but we also believe he is powerful from how he holds himself and moves, from the quality of his brooding stillness and the focus and clarity of his intention. We have a clear sense of his potential though it is only very occasionally demonstrated. This is true too of Giancarlo Esposito as Gus Fring in *Breaking Bad*, even though he has a small, delicate-looking frame. I am sure you can think of many others. As with both of these, we often recognise a person's potential for power in their stillness. We believe that they have learnt not to waste their energy, but that they will be swift and accurate if action is needed.

So we come back to working more skilfully, and to the grounded, centred place we explored in the previous Chapter. As Complicite's Marcello Magni says of Monika Pagneux: 'There are sequences of work that Monika does that propel you to move from immobility to great movement and to refined immobility. Calm, stillness, a centre.'[71] I would say that is also true of Feldenkrais lessons. You start somewhere, you find your way through a sequence of movements that might be very small or very big, and you come back to a different Home (or middle or centre), with a greater economy, a new equilibrium, a clearer grounding. You also experience a more refined integration (i.e. how everything works together) as well as differentiation (i.e. the ability to feel parts of yourself distinctly and separately). Your potential for power is visibly and actually enhanced.

We recognise the potential for power in movement as well as stillness: we read the balance and good organisation of someone's walk; the refined clarity and focus of a fully integrated gesture or action; the ability to vary and adapt behaviour as necessary. It is partly for the same reason: we clue into the signs that someone has the potential to carry out an action clearly and effectively in all kinds of circumstances. I suspect we are even designed to recognise someone who could be useful/protect us/do us harm, and someone who is no threat or not much use – and it makes sense from an evolutionary point of view. If so, that would mean that, if you want to be believable as powerful on stage, just trying to demonstrate some generalised or stereotyped idea of what you think powerful might look like probably won't wash. I don't mean you have to go into training – in these days of guns, bombs, computers and money, power isn't measured by physical strength anyway – but clarity of intention, the ability to act purposefully and effectively in changing circumstances, are skills you can learn. These qualities are always there to be read in how a person behaves and how they are. These skills are developed in any Feldenkrais lesson, where you are constantly asked to clarify and simplify the movement, looking for the most efficient, the most effective pathway. It can also be very clarifying in other ways: I gave a series of lessons to a medal-winning Paralympic sprinter with cerebral palsy, who told me that some days when her CP was 'playing up' her mind felt 'foggy', but after a Feldenkrais session it always felt clearer. This is not an uncommon response.

Because the approach in a Feldenkrais lesson is often slow and gentle, it is possible to miss how effectively the Method equips you for a physically powerful use of self too, but if you think of strength as a kind of skill it makes sense. Want to push or punch or kick or pull more effectively? There are many Feldenkrais lessons for the integrated use of legs and arms. Need better balance? Almost every lesson can help. Walking, running, twisting, throwing – you can find a lesson or approach to the action that will enable you to improve. There are lessons on squatting (which you need in many actions from jumping to weight lifting), on weight-bearing (on head or hands), and on many aspects of agility. Interestingly these are all movements essential to the kind of 'whole body' or functional strength-training that is becoming increasingly popular now. But I am going to bring out two strands that are particularly important when it comes to skills that enable power and the appearance of power: the use of the pelvis and the use of the head.

Moving from the Centre: The Power of the Pelvis

The classic centre of power is the pelvis. Martial artists and most sportspeople know it and use it. Just in simple muscular terms, you have the gluteal (buttock) muscles at the back of the pelvis, which are the biggest muscles in the body (in terms of diameter) and are the driving force (literally) in something like running. Then there is psoas, the powerful muscle which snakes through the pelvis from the leg right up into the lower back and pulls the leg up to the pelvis or tips the pelvis to the leg, and has a role both in moving and stabilising. And then there are the abdominal muscles that are attached around the rim of the pelvis, along with some significant movers of the trunk, like quadratus lumborum too. And that's just to name a few.

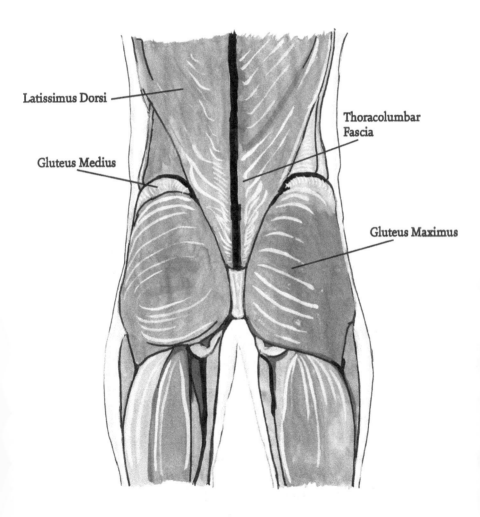

Latissimus Dorsi

Thoracolumbar Fascia

Gluteus Medius

Gluteus Maximus

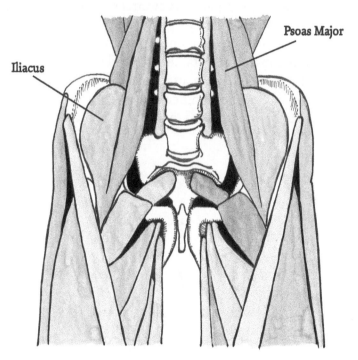

Some martial arts have what westerners would consider a rather mystical approach to channelling energy (or chi) through a place in the pelvic area called the tanden or dan tien, which coincides pretty much with the body's centre of gravity. Some have a more practical approach to simply organising the movement of the pelvis and use a mixture of tightening, bracing and releasing in this area for different purposes. Feldenkrais was a scientist as well as a martial artist, and, while some say his stance was changing towards the end of his life, his teaching was rooted in the very practical organisation and use of the pelvis.[72]

Those who do sports that involve throwing or hitting will know the power for the arms comes from the movement of the hips and support from the ground through the legs, and is carried from the pelvis through the trunk to the arms. Every baby who hasn't yet got a strongly developed musculature discovers that it needs to work out how to organise this heavy pelvis for any movement. A baby has to balance their big pelvis to stand and eventually to walk or it will sit down sharply. But as we grow up, too much sitting, too many imperatives about holding the abdominal muscles or keeping the pelvis still for social or aesthetic reasons – or according to some training methods – can diminish our ability to use it well. All too often we migrate away from the belly and into our heads.

Brain in Your Belly

Imagine your brain is in your lower belly instead of your head. That means everything you see or smell or hear is processed in your belly; every thought you have, every feeling is seated there.

Walk a little. Don't do anything special, don't demonstrate it so anyone can tell anything about what you are doing. Just 'know' that your brain is in your belly. It initiates every movement, makes every decision. Your head is just a passenger that collects some info, but it is not the big cheese any more than your hand or your leg. How does walking feel?

Do a few ordinary things like sitting down, standing up, opening a door. All with this sense that your brain is in your belly. What is the difference?

I am not saying your brain *is* in your belly (although if you look up what your guts actually do other than digest food, it's not as far away as you imagine), but it gives you a different feeling of yourself when you downgrade the head a bit and upgrade your 'powerhouse'. We will see in a minute why the movement of the head is, in fact, very important in organising movement, but it is not in any way a driver or a powerhouse. What muscles does it have to do anything like that with? Some people do punch with their neck/shoulder muscles when they are inexperienced. Not only does it limit movement possibilities by making the whole neck rigid and fixing the head in one place (and, in my experience, gives you headaches!), but it is no substitute for the power of the pelvis and legs.

For an actor, the ability to move from the pelvis is a large part of the process of finding a powerful presence on stage. It goes with grounding and centredness, and all those things that sound like voodoo when you first encounter them. They involve good use of the pelvis which, as a judo master, Feldenkrais was well placed to understand. There are a million lessons in the Method addressing the use of the pelvis. *The Pelvis Clock* is obviously one; here's another...

Lesson 8: Getting Up and Down from the Floor with a Twist

Stand, bend down and put your two hands on the floor. Bend your knees a little and walk your hands away from your feet a bit so you stand reasonably comfortably on hands and feet with your pelvis in the air...

Is it hard to do? If so come back up, bend your knees and put your hand on your legs just above your knees so you can lean on them like a backstop waiting for a catch. Now keep leaning on your legs with arms for support but lift your head and tail a little so your whole back arches and then lower your head and tail so your whole back rounds. One way your belly rolls out towards your thighs while your chest opens up at the front; the other way the belly moves in away from your thighs while your chest hollows. Notice how low down (towards the genitals) you can let the belly out or bring it in while allowing the movement to flow through your whole torso. Do it many times, softly and easily, paying attention to how the tailbone and head go up and down, and how your whole back moves in between.

Come back up to standing for a moment and then slide your hands down towards the floor again. Is it easier?

Let your knees bend as much as you need to take your hands to the floor and walk them forward so you can stand on hands and feet. Find where you can be comfortable with a distance between your hands and feet so you can even walk about a bit.

Stand up and have a rest whenever you need throughout this lesson.

Put both hands on the floor again in your comfy place. Now find how you can twist your right leg so that the knee can come towards the floor in the gap between the left foot and left hand. What do you have to do with the pelvis? That is the key here. Can you feel how it has to twist? The right side has to dip to help your leg move into the gap and you will find your whole back and chest has to twist, even though both hands stay on the floor. A mobile chest that can bend and twist like this is one of the most important, but least known, factors in full movement of the pelvis.

You may find that when the knee goes into the gap, you can think of placing the right side of the pelvis on the floor, and then, if you take the left hand away, you find you are sitting.

Replace the left hand and twist the pelvis back up into the air to reverse the movement. Stay on hands and feet and just whip the pelvis up into the air. Remember, a good movement is

reversible. Can you reverse it? One way the head goes down and the pelvis comes up, the other way the pelvis goes down and the head comes up. Like a see-saw. The spine and chest just follow. But it's the pelvis that leads. The head goes along for the ride on the end of the spine. Up and down. Remember the use of the ground. You have two arms and a leg whose contact with the floor via hands and foot can help you. Let the weight go down them into the ground as the pelvis twists up.

Come back to the same movement, but now make it light and quick. Just 'kiss' the floor with the right side of the pelvis and bring it straight back up on the rebound. As if you regretted going there. How do you get the movement light and quick? Have your focus on the pelvis: follow its trajectory down and pull it back up. Everything else will follow. The pelvis leads. But it can only lead if you are accurate about where it is going. Clarify it. Make it cleaner, simpler, lighter, faster. Move from the pelvis.

Try all this on the other side.

Now you have both sides working, you will find you can go from kissing the ground on one side to the other. But the speed and accuracy is all dependent on how you sink the pelvis and how you whip it back up, follow it around its circular motion to the other side and whip it back up. Pull the hip back and up. Your chest and back follow. That is the power of a well-organised pelvis. It is not about lots of effort and tightening: just about accuracy in where and how it is moving.

You may also find you don't need both hands on the floor, one is redundant. With only one hand on the floor you bring yourself into cross-legged sitting position, facing the opposite way to how you were standing. It's the same movement, but just using one hand and twisting a little further. The feet swivel a bit. You can go from standing, put one hand on the floor and twist the pelvis down to sitting and immediately back up, pelvis first and finally the head.

Try the opposite for a moment. Come back up by pulling the head up first and see what that does to the ease, lightness and speed of the movement, to the sense of everything moving together. Then, instead, keep the power and centre of the movement in the pelvis, and let the head just respond, rather than lead. How does this compare?

The irony, which I hope you appreciate, is that the movement is powerful and fast – but very, very light. Well-organised movement of the pelvis tends to have a speed and a lightness to it rather than the heaviness of unnecessary tension. And for an actor that is gold. An actor that drags themselves along by the head or chest won't have the lightness of an actor who can move from the centre. Of course, there can be a heaviness in the co-contraction of a forceful movement when impact is required. Of course, we can generate heaviness by succumbing to the gravitational pull or adding tension if we choose – if we want it, it can be there and it has its uses. But not as the only choice we have simply because we don't know how to organise the pelvis and move from the centre.

The Head (and the Eyes): Directing and Focusing Power

At the other end of the spine from the pelvis is the head. Like two balls on each end of a bendy pole. If the pelvis is the powerhouse, the head directs and focuses movement. I said you cannot create power from the head. It's true. It is no powerhouse in skeletomuscular terms. But it is hugely important in directing movement. Good movement of the pelvis, as you may have noticed in that lesson, helps to support and free the head, but the opposite is also true: fix the head in one relationship to the rest of you and you limit the possibilities of the pelvis – and much else too. It is a crucial player. A classic example of this limitation is when you ask a person to slide their hand down the outside of their leg and they leave their head upright on the spine rather than allowing it to tilt towards the shoulder and follow the movement to the side and down. Or just think of the times you have woken up with a crick in your neck and been 'plank person' for the day because you cannot move your head.

The Eyes Have It – Part 1

Stand and twist around to the right and notice how far you get.

Now twist around with the intention of seeing as far around you as possible. No doubt you went further. Here we start to notice that it is not just what the head does but also the organs in the head – especially the eyes.

Imagine you hear a noise behind you and turn so one ear is directed as far round behind you as you can. Different again.

The Eyes Have It – Part 2

'You know what you need at a crime scene? You need soft eyes. You got soft eyes you can see the whole thing. You got hard eyes you stare at the same tree missing the whole forest.'

Bunk in The Wire, *Season 4, Episode 4*

But there is more to it too...

Go for a walk in the room, let yourself have very relaxed eyes that sink a little in their sockets and a soft, wide peripheral vision that takes in as much of the room as you easily can. Allow your eyes to skim gently and take in the room as you go, without focusing strongly on anything. How does your head move if you don't stop it? What is the speed of your movement like? What quality does it have? Direct? Indirect, tense? Soft? How is your breathing?

Now focus your eyes on a point. The point may change or even sweep in an arc when you run out of space and need to change direction, but always you have a clear point of focus as you walk. What's the difference in the quality or even speed of your movement? What does your head do? How is your breathing? If you intensify the focus, what happens?

What you do with your eyes and your head affects the movement. It doesn't drive it, but it affects it strongly. At times in the last bit of this game you may have felt more or less powerful, or sensed different ways of being powerful. The actor's control of their head has a big effect on our sense of their potential power. For example, in one lesson at Oxford School of Drama working on the physicality of Greek tragedy (so all about economy and power), I was using that simple exercise of walking towards the audience and standing for a few seconds – but with a little more emphasis on the walk down towards the audience. One actor walked down towards us with his usual cowboy lope, but somehow didn't look as powerful to us as he clearly felt he was being, although it was hard to say exactly why. Then we put a neutral mask on him. Suddenly it was clear why: too much movement. In particular, one of the aspects of his cowboy walk was that his head swung through space left and right, and that just dissipated his focus and diminished his power. Everyone in the room agreed: there was far too much sideways movement away from centre, which looked unbalanced. I asked him what he could do to keep his head from swinging so much as we were losing the focus of the mask and any sense of power with it. He then found a walk that used more twisting around his central axis and less side-to-side bending so that his head could stay quieter, and suddenly there it was. Huge power and focus, like a stalking tiger in which everything moves around the centre and the head stays still, eyes unflinchingly focused. He took the mask off and he could still find that walk, so suddenly he had a new option which he really loved.

The opposite might also be true, the 'throwaway' of excessive movement in a cowboy walk can signal power: 'I am so tough I can be this wasteful and still be strong', or perhaps 'Hey, my thigh muscles/shoulders/balls are so big I have to move like this!' – but there is something devastatingly focused and powerful about the stillness of the head and the efficiency, balance and potential for speed inherent in twisting around the axis. When a tiger stalks everything else moves, but the head floats, allowing it freedom to turn and look anywhere, hear in any direction whatever the rest is doing. (The Bubishi again, principles no. 7 & 8 : 'The eyes do not miss even the slightest change. The ears listen well in all directions.') Again, this is about survival, and something deep in us recognises it. If your head is not free, you cannot tell as easily where danger is coming from, nor can you track dinner or focus swiftly where you need. The equivalent in modern life includes our ability to clock cars on the road; to anticipate the next punch in karate. But its effect on stage, and indeed life, is also to signal power. Stillness, focus and directedness.

Here is a great lesson for that kind of tiger movement.

Lesson 9: Twisting Around the Head

Walk a little and see if you can feel how your spine, chest and pelvis can turn even if your head doesn't. How much of a tiger can you be? How easily?

Stand now and just turn your head to see how easily you can look to left and right. Use more of you to look behind you and feel how it is. What places join in? If you improve your ability to move while your head remains comparatively still, the opposite should also be true: your head will be more free to turn as well.

Lie on the floor and notice your contact with the floor. Check through your legs, pelvis, back, ribs, shoulders, head... Does one side feel heavier or closer to the ground than the other in any places? As we saw before, sometimes we are already turning in one direction more than another.

Bend your right leg and plant the foot. Begin to press with this foot to roll the pelvis to the left as we did before on p. 125. The right side will lift a little while the left leans more. Go gently and slowly. Take out any unnecessary work or clenching in the abdomen. Think more of the pressing and leaning than the lifting. The lifting will take care of itself, it has the support of the ground. What part of your foot do you press with? Does your right knee travel to the inside? Can you find how to use more of your foot and keep the knee more towards the ceiling?

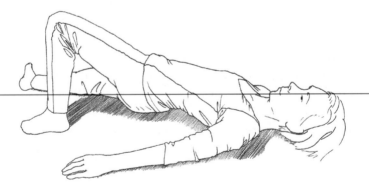

Keep pressing and rolling and coming back many times, but begin to direct the push a little higher so you can feel the lower back on the left come more to the floor. Then the lower ribs on that side, and so on working up the ribs, feeling each time how the turning can travel higher through the spine. Each time a place higher can lean on the floor, until you could even find the left shoulder.

Turn your head to the left as far as is comfortable and remind it to stay there by placing the back of the left hand on the right cheek and the back of the right hand in the palm of the left.

If it is not comfortable, find another way to gently pin your head and remind it not to move.

In this position, do the same pressing and rolling and feeling the movement travel through the spine as high as it can go. Notice how you match up the rest of the spine with the twist in the neck with the movement, and twist again on the way back.

Now turn your head to the right and pin it with your hands as before, but keep the legs the same and do the same pressing and rolling. But go gently. Each time you press and roll, you invite the spine to turn opposite to the head. Feel how high the turning can go without forcing or straining. Each time you come back you will be undoing the twist a little.

Do all these steps on the other side.

Bend both knees and plant both feet. Cross your knees, so the left leg hangs over the right, and turn your head to the right and pin it gently with your hands, as before. Let the knees move to the left. Feel how the foot tilts and the pelvis rolls. Gradually let the movement travel higher through the spine so that the knees come closer to the floor. Only where it is comfortable. Notice how the chest has to soften and twist.

Other side (head other side too).

Bend both knees up and plant the feet. Turn the head to the right and pin it, bring the right leg into the air with the foot towards the ceiling. Unbend the leg, but it doesn't have to be poker straight, just what is possible for you. Take the leg to the left.

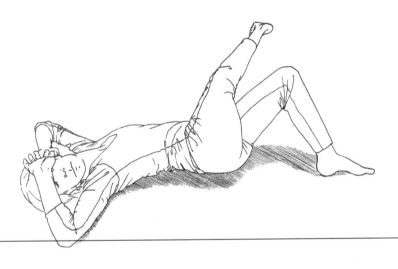

Find how you can use yourself to balance and not fall, how you can come back. Can the left knee stay more toward the ceiling? Eventually the right leg may come closer to the floor on the left, but don't force it to. It's just a direction, it doesn't ever have to touch. Feel how much of your back is involved, how high you need to move it for this.

Other side.

Bend your right knee and plant your foot and have the left leg long. Turn the head to the right and pin it. This time, imagine you could push something just an inch or two away with the heel of your left foot. Notice how you make the left leg longer. The bones can't get longer and tightening the muscles doesn't help so much. What can you do with the ribs and back and pelvis to help the whole left side get longer? See if you can find how to do it without arching your back away from the floor, let your back stay long on the floor (as if your back was a heavy length of rope that could lie on the floor) and lengthen through the whole side.

Do the same action, keeping your legs the same, but with your head turned to the left instead.

Both steps with the right leg long.

Notice how you rest on the floor at the end – any differences?

Stand and feel how it is. Turn your head and see how easily you can look to left and right. Use more of you to look behind you and feel how it is. What places join in?

Walk a little and see if you can feel how your spine, chest and pelvis can turn even if your head doesn't. Is it any easier, more fluid? How much more of a tiger can you be now?

Moshe Feldenkrais was interested in power and wrote a book called *The Potent Self*. His interest was not in being able to wield physical power over anyone else – although he was, of course, a skilled judoka. His idea of potency lay more in ability to make our own choices and do what we want effectively, without being dependent on or constrained by the ideas, opinions and approval of others (parents being the primary people we are initially dependent on, but also teachers, society, and so on). He described this state as being a fully mature human being, capable of independent thought, choice and action. As you work with the Feldenkrais Method you can start to feel how those dependencies, those inhibitions and difficulties, have shaped your very structure, your responses to the world. Just like that child in Part 1 who trains, internalises, normalises and habituates their range of responses to a parent that they are dependent on. A full discussion of this lies outside the scope of this book, but it is important to realise that, as an actor, your ability to be believably powerful on stage or screen is inevitably affected by these deep issues that can facilitate or inhibit your potential. I will talk more about this when discussing emotion in the next chapter, but you will find it is fundamental to all of Moshe Feldenkrais's thinking.

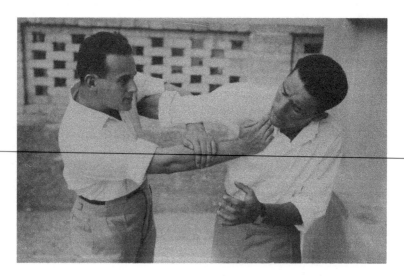

Moshe Feldenkrais in his early days: it is worth remembering that Moshe was a very strong man with a background that included street-fighting and judo.
© International Feldenkrais Federation Archive

Part 4

Emotion, Character and Creativity

4a. The Physiology of Emotion

For actors, being as emotionally open as they need to be for some roles can be a big issue. As Ute Hagen says, sometimes the kinds of feelings the actor is more used to and feels comfortable with are reasonably accessible, but when the actor feels under pressure to produce something less familiar or more extreme it can get difficult.[73] And, of course, in the business, conditions are not necessarily conducive. I have my own experiences that I know most actors will recognise, such as being required to break down in a scene on a long-running television series where the regulars were so bored they were playing jokes on the crew until the moment the camera rolled; doing the same show on stage over a long period; or playing a romantic scene on green (blue in those days!) screen with your scene partner represented by a cross on a stick. How do you find something that is believable, appropriate and effective in whatever way it needs to be in each situation? Every time. You can sometimes experience a rush of spontaneous feeling that seems powerful or 'true' and that connects with the audience, but for many such a feeling is random or even elusive.

The focus of acting teaching and techniques tends therefore to be on how to trigger an emotional response that reads as 'true' (without being overwhelmed or losing the context of what is needed for the scene) and on what you can do to find it – and find it repeatedly. There are methods that many actors find extremely useful in that arena, while others just find their own blend or their own way. I am not in the business of proposing a particular acting technique – and I can appreciate the benefits of many diverse acting theories – but I would like to look at what is involved in emotions and feelings, and how the Feldenkrais Method can facilitate a better understanding for an actor to enhance whatever process works for you.

Mental or Physical?

In my experience, the idea that feeling or emotion is purely or primarily a mental act (something that happens in your head) is still a prevalent 'common sense' view. It doesn't take much to point out that when you are sad, you cry, and when you are happy, you laugh – but these are often seen in a very limited way as physical manifestations secondary to a fundamentally mental state. As an actor you need a better understanding in order to be more emotionally available on stage, whenever you need. In every feeling state – whether that means the big emotions like anger, sadness, euphoric happiness, fear, anxiety, or the little fluctuations we make between alertness and relaxation, nervousness and confidence, contentment and dis-ease – there are shifts and changes throughout your physiology affecting breathing, heart rate, blood flow, the tonus of muscles, guts, and even sometimes the immune system.

The Sensation of Emotion

Stand and listen to how you are for a moment. Pay attention to your sensations – the tensions you can currently feel in yourself, where your weight is on your feet and how you are breathing – so you would notice if something changed.

Bring up a memory of something that made you angry (not overwhelmingly, just enough to do this and come out of it easily) and notice what alters in the musculature of your face, your neck and shoulders, chest, belly, legs. What alters in your breathing, your heart rate, in the way you give your weight to the ground? Let the feeling go and feel what shifts back again as you do so (sometimes easier).

Bring up something sad and notice what alters (again do not seek to be overwhelmed – just a taste). You may have more tension or less tension, lightness or heaviness, a different quality to your breath or other kinds of shifts to listen to. And listen to what reverts when you let it go.

It is usually enough to feel these emotions physically to understand what I am saying, but more subtle changes happen with every slight shift in mood, and if you train yourself to listen you will hear them in finer detail. There are other physiological changes happening that you cannot feel, but you can at least pay attention to the sensations that are available.

There is still no cut-and-dried explanation of the exact mechanics of emotion, and more and more factors are being recognised as significant, but over time the model has shifted towards a complex but holistic combination of neurophysical and mental processes.

It has also been established that the physical aspects of emotion are not necessarily subsequent to mental activity. In fact, it might be the other way around: butterflies in the stomach remind us we are nervous or excited; a sick feeling or racing heart tells us we are anxious or fearful. The physical aspect of emotion is obviously useful for communicating how we are feeling to others, but feelings and emotions also alert us to situations and conditions that we need to take notice of as calls to action for our protection and survival:[74] fear, anxiety and nervousness direct us away from danger or invite caution; pleasure and excitement direct us towards something for our well-being; anger and confidence enable us to face difficulty and danger or ward it off. Indeed, the word emotion is derived from the Latin '*e*', meaning 'out of, away from', and '*movere*', meaning 'to move'. Often a strong emotion can only be discharged through activity, be it running, fighting, throwing, speaking one's mind, crying, laughing, singing, dancing, making love or whatever.

The understanding of emotion as a physical event has been explored by thinkers from Charles Darwin through William James, Antonio Damasio, Nico Fridja and more, and is now widely accepted. Frijda states: 'Emotions are… matters of the body: of the heart, the stomach and intenstines, of bodily activity and impulse. They are of the flesh and sear the flesh. Also they are of the brain and the veins.'

And Moshe Feldenkrais asks:

> Which comes first – the motor pattern or the feeling? The question has been the object of many famous theories. I stress the view that basically they form a single function. We cannot become conscious of a feeling before it is expressed by a motor mobilisation, and, therefore, there is no feeling so long as there is no body attitude.[75]

At least one idea about acting is that it involves a kind of transparency: the actor transmits what they feel on the inside to the outside, and the actor's physicality needs to be fluid enough to enable that: not to create blocks. This dualistic image works and can be useful in a simple sense. An actor does indeed 'make visible the invisible', as Peter Brook suggests. One could go further and say there is no inside to outside, it is all one thing. Each feeling, each emotion, each current that passes through us is a unified event of the whole person. There has also been a far more facile argument over the years that has sought to separate actors who work from the 'outside in' from those who work from the 'inside out'. Perhaps we can finally lay that false dichotomy to rest.

> I... say that there is no identity. I say there is only one thing. There is a functioning nervous system inside, and that functioning has two aspects. If you listen to someone, you see the motor aspect and you also perceive the mental aspect (the content of his words). Any change in the nervous system translates itself clearly through a change of attitude, posture and muscular configuration. They are not two states but two aspects of the same state.
>
> *Moshe Feldenkrais*[76]

Whatever the exact mechanics and dynamics of how we experience emotions – which are still being argued over and pieced together in our brave new age of neurophysiology – the total involvement of a person's system in an emotional event is not in doubt.

Habits of Feeling

Feldenkrais said he was after more flexible minds, not more flexible bodies. Given the unity of mental and motor expressed above, he argued that it was easier to enable a person to change as a result of the shifts that occur spontaneously while exploring movement and sensation, rather than through an intellectual approach which directly engages a person in their habitual responses and patterns of thought. Over the years of doing Functional Integration (the hands-on technique in the Feldenkrais Method), I have learnt to see and feel under my hands the way a person's sensory-motor patterns are part and parcel of their emotional habits – their view of themselves and the world, their expectations, their habitual responses, their persistent patterns of feeling – some more enabling, some more disabling, depending on their experiences of life. I may not know the actual 'story' of what happened or have a hotline to their thoughts, but I can feel their patterns of tension and breathing. It goes back yet again to the baby in Part 1 and will recur in Part 4b to come. We learn our ways of moving, our ways of feeling and being, and our patterns of responding (be they physical or emotional), all together. It's complex and individual, and there is no instruction book of 'this means that' and 'that means that' – but you can see and feel the difference in breath, in muscle tone, in stance, even in someone's eyes and voice when there is a shift in how they feel. And vice versa, when the person senses a physical shift, the way they are feeling almost always shifts with it.

An extreme example is a very intelligent young man who came to see me who had a history of anger and violence that was serious enough to have landed him in prison. Although always polite to me, his past was very present in the high level of tension he carried: in his hawkish posture, his swift, sharp movements, his piercing gaze and his hyper-alert state. I only knew fragments of his story but I could see and feel it too. The few Feldenkrais sessions we did brought his system into a place where he looked more upright, more open and softer, and he was able to feel more at one with himself and at ease. He told me with pleasure that after a session people didn't cross the road when they saw him coming; that a woman had even initiated a conversation with him at the bus stop; and that he didn't feel the same need to get angry with his neighbour.

So perhaps we can say we have habits of feeling as much as we have habits of moving, breathing, speaking and holding ourselves. Some of us, like this young man, can fall into a pattern of anger easily, but perhaps not a pattern of tenderness or of sadness. Others may find anger almost impossible to access. As Ute Hagen says, familiar and/or less threatening feelings and emotions will be easy for an actor to access and use. Others are not so familiar – not so habitual, we could say – or feel threatening in some way, and so are harder to access. Her suggestion is to recall a time when such an emotion was felt and seek for the associated sense (affect) memory (the associated smell or sound or small visual detail perhaps) that escaped the 'censor' (the part of yourself that has repressed it), and so could trigger the release of the emotion that has been repressed. Memory is indeed not stored all in one place in the brain but in many places in relation to our senses, any piece of which can bring the whole flooding back, including its emotional content. But some feelings can be very well defended, depending on the person's life experiences, and we have to respect that that might actually be for very good reasons. As our patterns of feeling are part and parcel of our motor patterns, it's also possible to approach them through the sensory-motor system without having to remember events of any kind, and it can happen without directly trying. Some of the habits of tension (or 'holding') that we learn to recognise and open up through Feldenkrais lessons, are likely to be part of defensive patterns which will gradually loosen their compulsive grip. This happens as it becomes safe to do so, because other more functional patterns become available and eventually preferred. In this way it often happens that a wider palate of feeling and emotion becomes safely available too. It can simply help with whatever other process you are using too.

For an actor, using Feldenkrais to develop a more sensitive, more fluid system, less bound by compulsive habits, is also likely to be enabling in terms of allowing emotional or mental shifts. It doesn't mean if you can do the splits you are a higher form of life – let's be very clear about that – because I am not talking about that kind of flexibility. It means if you are able to feel, allow, adapt and respond in a variety of ways, not just in limited compulsive habitual patterns, it will affect your emotional and mental potential. I will have more to say about how reason and thinking are shaped by movement and our bodily sensation in Part 4b, but all of it harks back to that very first example of the baby in Part 1. How we learn to move and sense ourselves is shaped by our experience as well as our genetic make-up. By extension, how we learnt to move and sense ourselves – our self-image – will keep shaping how we think, feel and experience ourselves and the world. That's the big picture that Feldenkrais addresses, and another reason why it is such a fruitful study for an actor who wishes to bring to life another character's way of thinking, feeling and experiencing themselves and the world.

Everything we have seen so far in terms of working with patterns and habits applies here too. As well as asking how you can make an emotion come up, you can also why it isn't coming up – what is getting in the way. Once again you can ask what you can do *less* in order that you have more available as an actor.

Most of the great teachers and theoreticians came to the same conclusion as Stanislavky, that: 'muscular tautness interferes with inner emotional experience'.[77] For instance, here is Michael Chekhov: 'Every actor, to a greater or lesser degree, suffers from some of the body's resistance';[78] or Sanford Meisner: 'Neutral: what does that mean? Open to any influence right? If you are neutral you will achieve a kind of emotional flexibility won't you? If you're tense, if you're unrelaxed, you're not responsive.'[79]

Many teachers and theoreticians have their versions of 'relaxation' exercises to get around the problem of habitual tension. However, 'relaxation techniques' or stretching exercises, while helpful, are sometimes too general to address our very deep unconscious patterns of holding, especially when it comes to the ones that involve emotional responses. The Feldenkrais Method offers some more sophisticated options.

There is a sense in which tension is part of feeling. The level of tension you feel when you are excited or angry, alert, depressed, determined, frightened or contented is different because the motor aspect of all these emotions is different. (Jacques Lecoq's 'Seven Levels of Tension' plays with this idea going from being almost inert with flaccidity to being immobilised by tension, each of which suggest a different way of being.) In terms of emotion, some aspects of tension are not really part of the emotion itself but result from the effort we use to stop the feeling flowing into action – or even to stop the feeling itself. Here is a version of a Stanislavsky exercise that illustrates this.

Feeling and Tension

Stand for a moment and bring up a memory of some tender moment. Someone you love arriving or departing, or some gentle, happy or nostalgic time. Listen again to the kinds of changes in your physicality that you can perceive, as in the previous game. Listen very carefully. Now let it go and listen to what reverts.

And now imagine you are on the motorway with a couple of mates and you have a puncture. The tyre has to be changed, but your friend (whose car it is) doesn't have a jack. Two of you will have to hold the car up while your friend changes the tyre (yes, it's possible, I've been in this situation on tour!). Do the action of lifting the car. It's very, very heavy. You have to make a great effort and strain hard. While you are in that state of immense strain, try to bring up the soft tender feeling you had a moment ago. Can you do it? Let the car go.

Unless you are a well-trained martial artist who doesn't include tensing and straining in their image of lifting the car, you most likely struggled to bring up the tender emotion. Notice that it's not just that you couldn't portray it at the same time as straining, it is very likely that you couldn't even feel it. I've done this many, many times with many groups and the result is always the same. So now: 'Which comes first, the motor pattern or the feeling?'

To come back to our one event that is both mental and physical at the same time, it may not be the case that the feeling is inside but blocked and so can't travel from inside to outside: it may not be to do with the actor's transparency and not being seen from the outside – it may be that it *can't be felt at all*. When you are sad or frightened and you want to cry or scream, what is it that you do to stop the sadness or fear? One way is to tighten up to stop the physiological process, so that all you can feel is the tension of the muscles in your chest or diaphragm or stomach or wherever, and not the sadness or the fear. It is that strain and effort that we see when we say someone is 'holding something in', but as in straining to lift the car, the tension is more likely to be stopping it happening at all. Another way is almost the opposite: a sort of frozen limpness where mind and body are not engaged – a kind of dissociation like an animal playing dead. Both involve an inappropriate level of muscular work and stop the feeling happening, in the same way that blocking your ears stops you hearing or closing your eyes stops you seeing.

A final example: what do you do to stop yourself being angry? If you can't let it out in some active way, you might try and reason yourself out of it – and if you are successful you will feel all the physical effects subside. However, you might well hold yourself even tighter to suppress the feeling. If you can, you might take deep breaths and let go of the tension, in which case the softening is likely to take away not just the display of anger, but the anger itself.

Sometimes the way you suppress the emotion is a conscious choice even if the mechanism isn't. Sometimes it happens without you even trying or perhaps knowing, because your system senses it is not safe or that you could be overwhelmed. The latter is part of the mechanism that comes into play in serious trauma and post-traumatic stress disorder, but you can also see it when people say 'it hasn't hit me yet', in those moments you swallow or shelve the little insults and upsets of the day because it is just not useful or the right moment to allow yourself to feel or deal with them – and then you just never actually come back to deal with them. Indeed, you may not even notice you do it.

What does all this mean for you as an actor? It means you have patterns of holding tension that affect your movement and also have to do with controlling emotion. It means excessive strain and effort get in the way of finding easy, fluid, nuanced patterns of *feeling*, as well as moving. It means that if you dig deep and wind yourself up, pushing yourself to find a pitch of emotion you think you need for a scene, you are likely to add more tension and actually make it harder for yourself to feel anything (as Ute Hagen would agree). In addition, as we saw in the section on *complicité*, the tension and the internal effort may cut you off from what is really going on between you and the other actors in the scene – which, ironically, is likely to be the very source of what truly enables the flow of something appropriate to the moment. The emotional tenor of the scene is not just your responsibility and a result of your internal work alone, but grows in the space between the actors when there is openness, connection and *complicité*. So ultimately it means that once your compulsive patterns lose their grip a little – once you can develop alternatives and a wider range of possibilities, once you can safely be more open – all you need is to know the circumstances of your character and the scene, and be fully present with the other actors in order to open up the space for whatever is needed to flow between you – be that jokes, tears, anger or tenderness.

I mentioned earlier Feldenkrais's notion that when you only have one option you are an automaton; two and you are at the level of a light switch; more than two and you become human. Clearly, 'human' is where an actor needs to be. Once they have come out of the initial trance-like state some Feldenkrais lessons can induce, actors can often access themselves and be more emotionally open and responsive to others. A Feldenkrais lesson lowers the overall level of intensity. It provides support in the system to lower the defences enough for something to happen.

It allows the actor to take the foot safely off the brake.

There is research becoming available on this idea. Norman Doidge notes: 'When people feel safe, the parasympathetic nervous system turns off the fight-or-flight reaction';[80] and as Stephen Porges has brilliantly demonstrated, the parasympathetic system also turns on a 'social engagement system'[81]... allowing people to listen to, communicate and connect with others. Sounds like *complicité* to me.

Think back to the client I mentioned earlier. He was used to people in the street avoiding contact with him and yet after a lesson that was no longer true.

Ebb and Flow

Through learning to listen to yourself with increasing accuracy during Awareness Through Movement Lessons (should you pursue the Method), you can learn to feel those shifts and changes in breathing, heart rate and muscular tone, and it can form a background awareness against which you can navigate through a play or find the moment in front of a camera. We discussed awareness in Part 2, which is not a self-consciousness, but a connectedness to what is going on inside you. It also enables you to sense the ebb and flow of the 'currents' of feelings and emotions within you: once you have a sense of the shape of those currents in a scene or even a whole play, something in you will seek it, shape it from within as you go through the performance. I can still recall Rose of Sharon's empty despair towards the end of *Grapes of Wrath*, which I played thirty years ago. But as I remember the scene, what I notice is the sensation in my belly, chest, jaw and throat – down my arms, behind my eyes and what it does to my breathing. Even now. And with that physical sense comes the emotional sense of it. Very different to the feeling of her earlier in the play: perky, spoilt and newly married – a light, bright, full, sensual, hips-and-lips kind of sensation. It's not that I didn't do other kinds of actor prep too, but once I was actually on stage, the changing physical map was always there in the background. Along the same lines, Michael Chekhov invites the actor to take on a physical shape or gesture to find the essence of a character or of a moment, and Ute Hagen invites the actor to become alive to all their senses. Back then I didn't use either as a formal technique (in fact, I had never heard of them!), but I still had a sense of the ebb and flow, the shifting shapes and physical feel of the character's emotional journey. Feldenkrais can do a great deal to tune you in to that possibility.

Reversibility

Once you can sense the physical flow and shape of your states of feeling, it also becomes easier to reverse and switch in and out without getting stuck somewhere. Pretty useful for an actor. I once worked with an actress who used to tell jokes in the dressing room until a few minutes before she went on, then come back in at the end of a highly emotional scene, wiping away tears and running mascara and get straight back to the jokes before her next equally emotional scene. She could do it every time. And most of the (experienced, talented, respected) cast in one long-running play that I was in used to watch *Casualty* on TV in the green room between scenes, and then go on and give fabulous performances. At the time, I couldn't understand how on earth they could do it. Sometimes young actors – especially students –fall headlong into an emotion, playing it for all they are worth, and end up apparently unable to come out of it. There is a real danger of falling in love with being carried away like this and thinking it's the 'real deal' – that we must torment ourselves and 'give our all' – but, as actors become more experienced, they understand that it is the audience who are meant to have the experience, not them: just because an actor felt the earth move, doesn't mean the audience did. In fact, quite the opposite sometimes: the actor disappears into a welter of emoting, stumbles off into their own corridor and ends up losing the audience and pulling the play apart.

Reversibility gives you the facility to shift, change, go in and out, modulate and allow just what is needed to happen – no more, no less. You can play this next game in different ways: go into it slowly and out of it fast, or into it fast and out of it slowly, until you have acquired ease and facility.

As with a Feldenkrais lesson, using just a bit less will give you a better learning experience than trying for something too big. If you are not sure how it will go, make sure someone is with you, so long as you don't *perform* it for them!

Grading and Reversal of Emotion

Listen how you feel as you stand. Listen to your breathing, heart rate, level of muscle tension in different places, and where your weight is.

Now think of some moment in your past when you were very happy, but don't go there yet.

Take five slow steps forward and allow yourself to let that feeling of happiness grow, sensing what changes physically as you go. Allow it to change you physically even if it is not naturalistic. Time it so that you are at the peak of the feeling when you get to step five and stay there for a moment, allowing yourself to feel what it is like: what shape the feeling forms you in to, where your weight is, how your breathing feels, where your level of tension is now. Then take five steps backwards, undoing the physical feeling and shape gradually until the emotion is also gone.

Do the same thing over ten steps, so you have to allow the feeling to grow even more slowly. Stay in contact with the growing physical sensation and shape of it. Then take ten steps back, allowing the physical sensation and shape of the emotion to undo themselves until it is all completely gone.

Try the same with sadness or tenderness, and, if you are feeling brave, you can even try anger. If you do, don't allow tension to hold the anger back too much, but be careful. Don't pick any memory that could be remotely overwhelming, and stay anchored in your physical sensation. It is very important to be able to take those ten steps back again just as carefully, meticulously undoing the physical sensation completely and noticing how the emotion goes away totally with it. The lesson is all about reversibility and absolutely not about getting stuck in your emotion and showing off how much you can 'feel'.

4b. Character and Creativity

(The) very structure of reason itself comes from the details of our embodiment.

Internet Encyclopaedia of Philosophy, 2005

Character

Feldenkrais is a fabulous tool if you are thinking about character, since, as you discover more possibilities in yourself, new ways of moving and being are more likely to emerge as you play. It also becomes more possible to find new patterns by observing and stealing them from other people, because your ability to *feel* differences in yourself will also allow you to begin to *see* the differences in others much more accurately. That in turn enables you to try out their way of being more accurately and in a more integrated way (as opposed to pasting bits of it on like a false beard). Eventually this may not necessarily be a case of consciously copying (useful as that can be for learning and exploring) but may come about because something appropriate emerges in the moment. The thing to remember is that only what is available in you can emerge. If it is not available it can't. Simple as that. Hence all the Feldenkrais work, which enables you to have as much available as possible for the moment you need it.

Okay. That's going to take a little more explaining to be clear.

What Makes a Character?

We could say that a character is just a person revealed through their behaviour in a series of situations. They are the kind of person who speaks, acts, behaves and responds as written in the text, and that's all. As a result of the contraction of time, the concentration of events and the focus on humour or drama in a play or film, either the character or the situations faced or both may tend to the extreme. However, it is still essentially a person seen in a variety of situations, so that if you play what is there in the writing and in the moment, the character should be revealed (it depends on how well written the script is, of course). And it also depends on what you have in your toolbox and in your range of play.

Given this definition of character, we can remind ourselves that every person learns their own patterns and habits of movement from birth (as in Part 1), and that developing ways of feeling, experiencing, responding to and acting in the world is tied in with learning to move (as in the previous chapter). We have already seen that this means that every person's movement patterns are an intrinsic part of their emotional and behavioural patterns. We have also seen that each person learns all this in an environment that includes the people they are brought up by and the values of the wider community, as well as the positive and negative experiences they have, the activities they are drawn towards or not, and so on. We have seen how all these aspects of each person's history (and more) are part and parcel of the quality and range of movement they have and how they hold themselves, and we saw this is not so much a duality of mind and body as an integrated whole.

All *this* is the stuff of character. You can see, therefore, that understanding the society, the background and whatever can be gleaned of the personal history and relationships of a character is important in many kinds of play and film – hence the historical or social research most actors do; the analysis of the character's situation, their desires, motivations and strategies and other characters' attitudes and responses to them. However, there is a danger in actors 'working on their character' alone, elaborating on the text, making decisions and then playing some intellectual idea of the character they have developed in their head. An actor also crucially needs to discover what all the above means for how they behave in the moment, respond to the other actors, inhabit their skin, breathe, move. It is an argument for discovering by doing, playing and trying out, all of which is also fundamental to the Feldenkrais Method. In addition, awareness of self and development of skill through movement will make a significant difference to the quality and detail of characterisation that an actor may be able to find.

As I said in the Introduction, Feldenkrais pointed out that movement is fundamental to everything – indeed, there is no life without it. If you have ever seen a corpse you will know what he is saying. The stillness is shocking. The movement of breath, blood flow, digestion, the constant level of work in the muscles, the ripples and shifts that are so unremarkable in a person at rest are startling in their absence in death... Movement *is* life. Not just the external trappings, the picture-postcard, sign-posted version of a person's movement, but the feel, the muscular tone, the rhythm, the quality, breath and pulse of this person; and the detail of how they negotiate their way through the world, down their street, across their kitchen. How they mould themselves to meet their life. To fit it.

Discover this within the context of the text and you have most of the character. Find it from playing the text, or from the games you play with the text, or around the text – or however you like to do it. If you have no text because your project is to be devised, then you can work the other way around – movement first and then find out about the sort of person who moves like that. You can go backwards and forwards or any way around till you get there. As long as you understand that who and how you are, and how you move and behave, are part of the same thing.

> The embodiment of reason via the sensorimotor system... is a crucial part of the explanation of why it is possible for our concepts to fit so well with the way we function in the world. They fit so well because they have evolved from our sensorimotor systems, which have in turn evolved to allow us to function well in our physical environment.
>
> *Lakoff and Johnson*[82]

Self-image

The opening sentence of Feldenkrais's book, *Awareness Through Movement*, talks about the same thing: 'We act in accordance to our self-image. This self-image – which, in turn, governs our every act – is conditioned in varying degree by three factors: heritage, education and self-education.'

Let's look at this statement in detail: 'self-image – *which, in turn, governs our every act*' is an enormously powerful thing to assert about us as human beings, and very significant for actors and what they can play. How differently and specifically you can mould yourself to the character also depends on how much your self-image can contain. For instance, if I can only see myself as the little bird person my slight frame suggests, and if I have strongly invested in that image of myself, then I will move all the parts of myself like the tiny fragile thing I have identified myself with: that's how I will be seen, what I will bring to every role and how I will be cast. If I have found that I can move differently in a way that gives me an experience of myself as powerful, strong and resilient, then I will have that other possibility available – but only if I can actually welcome and contain that image of myself and not reject it as too strange, unfamiliar, threatening to my way of life and relationships, or just 'not me'. It interests me how many ways of moving and being an actor willingly rejects because they do not want to own that possibility. It's really normal to reject things, but it's very interesting that we do in this situation. I see it all too often in my drama-school students at the end of a lesson. Sometimes they love what they have just found, but sometimes they respond with: 'Oh, it feels weird, I don't like it!'

A while ago I had struggles with the requirement to stamp in certain karate movements. I couldn't work out how to do it in some more demanding positions, like at the end of a long lunge along with an elbow strike. I shifted my weight very carefully and placed my foot softly, even elegantly. 'No,' said Sensei Kevin. 'Stamp! Don't be so delicate. Stamp. You are meant to be stamping on someone's foot. Stamp! Strong. And *kiai* [shout]!' I tried. I failed. I wanted to do it right, and it's not like it's a very hard movement. I knew I needed to shift my weight forward quicker so it was over my foot. Hell, every kid knows how to stamp. *I* know how to stamp! But something in me held me back, got in the way of letting me work out the timing of shifting weight to allow me to stamp. Something in me did *not* want to own this stamp. I didn't want to feel the jarring quality of the movement. I didn't want to bang the ground. I didn't want to contain that possibility. I didn't want to be the person that stamps or be seen that way. I wanted to tread lightly. Being able to tread lightly is great. Stamping and banging around is not a good mode of being most of the time: not for joints, not for the world. But there are times when it is just the thing you want, and to limit myself like that is… well, a shame.

There may be ways of being and possibilities that you just don't want to explore or contain – actors get asked to go to some pretty extreme places, after all – or there may be roles that are just too far away to be a reasonable ask. No one can play every character. I will only be the fighter I can be within what is possible for me. I won't be Sensei Kevin Goodman or Sensei Linda Marchant, or even the person of my own grade next to me in training. But I can contain a wider or narrower image of me.

I can be more or less 'me'. As an actor, you can have more or less to play with. Often actors chose to stick to a narrow path, not just in the characters they play but even in the responses they give. It's very understandable in the context of the business. But Feldenkrais offers you a safe way to experience something that might enable you to break out – or edge out – of those limits.

Observation of Self and Others

We have seen that, to know or mould yourself to anyone else's movement, you must first know your own, since if you have no idea of your starting point, you cannot know how it could be different. Once you get a sense of the different ways you can be, you can also start to recognise the range of possibility in others. It is at this point I like to ask students to analyse what they can see in other people. If you have just done a lesson that clarifies for you some of the different ways you can use your leg in relation to the rest of you when you walk, you are more likely to be able to see which of those possibilities someone else prefers to use. Then you can notice that what you read from them contributes to any judgement you make about their character. For example, we have seen in Part 3b that, when you shift weight from one leg to the other in walking, whether you swing your head through space or leave it more or less in the middle, makes a difference to our sense of you. But there are a million details in walking. It is extraordinarily complicated. Change one detail in the way you use your toes, your eyes, your shoulders, your jaw, even your wrists when you walk, and you will read differently to the audience. It can be difficult to work with this without it being self-conscious, mannered or tagged-on, unless you have a considerable wealth of choice available to you so that a deeper response can simply emerge in the moment. We are not talking about 'silly walks'; rather, the job is to make as much available in your system as possible; to recognise difference and play with it so that you can trust it to turn up appropriately without 'playing' it, as such. Here we are back to 'techniques happen in the absence of conscious thought' (the Bubishi) and the discussion of awareness in Part 2. As I have already said, only what is available in you can actually turn up. If it's not there, it can't. And that's where Feldenkrais comes in.

Feldenkrais in this context is a tool many actors learn to love. It is utterly fascinating to have clearer ways of actually seeing what is going on: an infinite set of filters through which you can feel what you do, then see what someone else is doing and use it to inspire ways to find new versions in yourself.

Here is a very simple practical example to illustrate this.

Relocating Your Hip Joints

Put your fingers on where you think your hip joints are. Hip joints, not hip bones, i.e. where you think the top of the thigh bone actually meets (articulates with) the pelvis. If you do this in a group of people they will often have quite different ideas.

Go to p. ii and look at the picture of the skeleton, and the picture of the pelvis on p. 107. When attempting to locate their hip joints, some people will touch the top rim of the pelvis known as the iliac crest (think of the stereotypical 'hands on hips' stance when someone is cross). Some will put their hands lower down on the outside of the leg at the widest point of the hips. This makes some sense, as you can feel that place moving when the leg moves. It is part of the thigh bone, but is actually the outer-most point of the bone called the 'greater trochanter', from which the leg bone then does a sharp turn inwards (and still a little upwards) deep inside the groin, where the hip joint actually is.

To find where your hip joints really are you can put your hands on the foremost edge of the iliac crest and then run your fingers down the crease of the groin towards the lowest mid-point of the genital area (or where the two pubic bones meet in the middle). Roughly halfway down that line, but a fair way inside you, are the hip joints (have another look at the pictures). They are much closer to your midline and deeper inside you than you may have imagined: as close to the back of you as they are to the front. You might have appreciated this in *Lesson 5: The Pelvic Clock* and, if you didn't, it is well worth doing that lesson again with this new awareness, as it will be a different experience.

So now we can play a game with it.

Imagine your hip joints are indeed at the iliac crest, the top rim of the pelvis. Now walk as if your legs join and move from here. Make it as normal as you can. One way is to start by exaggerating to get it then do less and less until the idea is still there, but you are not overdoing it. How does it feel? What does it do to other parts of you – how you hold yourself and move overall? Who is this person? How do they relate to the world?

Now shift your imaginary hip joints to the outside of your legs at the widest point of the hips – the greater trochanters. Walk as if your legs are jointed here. Make it more subtle, more normal; allow the rest of yourself to join in so as to make it possible. Ask yourself the same questions.

And now deep in the groin where they really are. How is this different? (Have another look at the pictures to be clear.)

In fact, you can move them all over the place – try locating your hip joints somewhere obviously impossible like your armpits or the back of your neck. You may find some interesting things. You can exaggerate or you can bring it right down to just a hint of the idea.

This is interesting in more than one way. Firstly, it illustrates how your idea of yourself affects how you move, otherwise how could you change the way you walk by simply imagining you have relocated your hip joints when they actually stay in the same place? But secondly, now you have felt these different possibilities in yourself, it gives you a way into seeing and trying out where other people think their legs are jointed and how they use them.

Where Do Other People Have Their Hip Joints?

Next time you are in the street, watch a few people carefully (don't be obvious or they won't like it). Where do they think their hip joints are? Where do they move their legs from? What does it make you feel about them as a result? It is only one aspect of the person, so don't expect it to affect them all the same way or to be able to make any rule about it. Just get an eye for the range. If you start looking and working like this you will soon see other aspects of what makes one person different from another.

Planes of Movement

This is just one little idea: where people move their legs from is influenced by more factors than this. Walking is very complex, and you could use many of the lessons in the Feldenkrais Method to sensitise yourself to the ways all the different parts of you can be involved – the above is just a quick taste: the lessons contain far more detail.

For example, one set of filters I use is 'planes of movement'. If you go back to *Lesson 5: The Pelvic Clock*, there are two main planes that the pelvis – and so the whole spine – is moving in: tipping the pelvis up and down to 12 and 6 creates bending and arching through the whole spine, while tilting left and right to 3 and 9 creates twisting.[83] The third plane (which replaces twisting if you do *The Pelvic Clock* sitting upright on a chair) is side-bending/lengthening.

These three planes together in different degrees make up the foundations of every movement we do. You can work with these planes in a myriad of ways in any number of Feldenkrais lessons to improve your own pelvic and spinal movements. As you develop a better sense of these planes and how they combine in day-to-day movements (like walking, reaching, pushing, pulling, lifting), you see how other people put their movements together – ways you could probably never conceive of for yourself! Some people walk in a cowboy style, mostly side-bending and swaying the chest and head. Some people side-bend or even translate lower in the hips (sticking the hip straight out to the side): a more stereotypically 'female' walk. Some people walk with a stronger arch in the lower back or a lifted chest; some with a rounded back, some go from one to the other more subtly in a kind of wave; some have a strong twist mostly down in the hips, some twist all the way through the back; some side-bend as they bring one leg through, and twist as they bring the other leg through. And there are as many varieties as people, especially once you add in rhythm.

I had fun with one actor who had to go from playing a cowboy in one film to playing a courtier at Versailles during the reign of King Louis XIV in another film. In the second film he needed to be believable both as a swordsman and as a proficient court dancer. We worked with the shift from his easy cowboy side-bending style of walking to being able to twist better. That way he could stay more upright around his central axis and keep his head quieter, both for greater poise and for the baroque style of movement he now needed. I had done a little to help that same actor improve his punch by working with the connection of his hip to his arm in a scene about a boxing match: twisting again.

Here is a lesson to help you feel that kind of twisting around the axis and where your leg moves from.

Lesson 10: Where Does Your Leg Move From?

Walk a bit. As I asked right at the start of the book, notice what happens when one leg goes forward. Does that side of your pelvis go forward too? Or backwards: in the opposite direction to your leg? Or does it stay quiet? What about your other leg?

Keep walking. What happens when one leg becomes the back leg? Has that side of your pelvis gone backward too? Or forwards: in the opposite direction to your leg? Or does it stay quiet? What about your other leg?

Do you feel any twisting movement in your back as you walk? If so, how high up your back do you feel it?

Lie on your front with your head to the right, your right arm on the floor but bent so you can see your hand. Bend your two knees so the soles of your feet are towards the ceiling.

Let your right foot lean against your left lower leg and begin to slide that foot down the inside of the left lower leg so that it pushes the left leg: both feet will travel to the left. Your knees don't slide on the floor. Then return. Make this movement many times and feel how it starts to invite your pelvis to turn, so that your belly rolls a little on the floor. Notice how high in your spine you turn to help with this movement of the legs. You may notice it by feeling some places in your front lean more on the floor or peel away from it.

Have a rest and then try the same movement on the other side: with your head to the left and legs going to the right.

In the original position, head to the right, put your legs (knees and ankles) close together, touching – as if they were tied together. Now tip your legs to the left again. Don't let them separate. What happens to your right knee? Can you feel how it has to leave the floor if you are careful not to let your legs separate by one sliding down the other? Go gently, but notice how high you start to turn in the spine now, and how much of your front changes its contact with the floor. Where are your legs moving from now?

Be careful: it is important to focus on exploring how the ribs and upper back can join in, otherwise your lower back could end up doing too much, which might become painful. Also listen to where your heels are. Notice that if you bring them closer to your buttocks, your lower back will arch more, so be careful that your knees stay more or less at a 90° angle and the movement is not 'cut off' by too strong an arch in your lower back. Also listen to your tailbone. If you start to stick it out, your back will over-arch and again the movement will get stuck there. Have a sense that you can lengthen the tailbone away and the front of the hips can open up to the floor as you roll. If it is not comfortable do it differently, or stop.

Do the same on the other side.

Come back to the original position, head to the right, legs close together, and this time plant your right hand as if for a push-up. As you tip the legs to the left again, feel how the pelvis turning and the legs going down to the side can help you lift your head and look over your right shoulder in the direction of your feet (you probably won't see them, it is just a direction). Your right hand is there to help and support, but see if you can find how the legs and pelvis are the motor for lifting your head rather than relying on your arms too much. Can you find how it could become all one movement? It could feel a little like a see-saw: legs go down as head comes up, then head up and legs down.

Other side.

This time plant both hands, head to the right. As your bent legs go to the left and you lift your head to look towards them, let the right leg slide even further back. It might be that the leg going back could carry you into sitting if you let one hand peel away, but spend some time just noticing where this leg is moving from: how much does the twisting and arching movement of your back (and lengthening of your front) enable this backward movement of the leg? Can you feel it even high in your chest? Maybe up to the base of your throat? Don't force it, just play with it.

Other side. You can also play with going from one side to the other!

Have a rest on your back. If you feel it is over-arched, bring your knees to your chest a few times.

Now stand up and walk again and see if you can feel this twisting motion in walking. Can you feel your pelvis move forward and back with your legs? How high in your back do you move now to allow your pelvis to turn and help your leg move? Stop your back and pelvis from moving and feel the difference. Now you can only walk from the hip joints. And now let your back and pelvis turn again. (Sometimes you can feel the twisting more clearly when you walk slowly backwards!)

You can also use *Lesson 9: Twisting Around the Head* to explore where your leg is moving from. Again you can notice how high up your back has to twist for your legs to go over to the side. In the very last part you can notice how high up in your ribs and spine your side has to lengthen for your leg to push away. Conversely, *Lesson 10* can teach us about the head – the original name of the lesson is 'The Carriage of the Head', because in it you find how the leg and pelvis help to bring the head upright as you come to sit.

Different Parts

You can also look at where people move most or what leads them. Some people seem to move most with their shoulders – or even their heads – dragging the rest of themselves around. Some people's chest or hips dominate. Sometimes almost nothing seems to move except somehow the feet and legs. This is familiar territory, I am sure, but when you get more specific about *exactly* where and how, and underpin it with a more subtle understanding of planes, it gets interesting.

For example, take the feet. Not only do people angle their feet differently by turning their toes/heels in or out and have them narrower or wider and so on, but their weight is distributed through different parts of the feet because of how they stand and walk: some people lean more on the inside or outside of heels, or the balls of the toes – or even on the balls of specific toes – or they might clench the toes or even lift them. Their choice will affect their entire gait.

Standing in the Sand

You need at least two or three people for this.

Fill a large (clean!) cat litter tray with sand (or head for the beach).

One person steps into the sand in bare feet and makes a clear set of prints in the sand. Then they step out again, careful to disturb the shape and depth of their prints as little as possible.

A second person then steps into those prints, very carefully matching their feet to the shape, angle and relative depth of the different parts of the prints. Matching the angle of the feet makes a big difference, but when you include the depth of the prints in this way, the second person has to adapt themselves to how the first person carries their weight. It is often a big shock to really feel how everything throughout their whole body has to change as a result – even how they hold their head. Jaws drop.

The second person then steps out of the box maintaining that posture and walks about like that to feel who this person is.

Whatever you feel when you step into someone else's prints isn't *really* how they feel, even though it may share something. It depends on how your system can adapt and what that brings up in you, but it is still a way into feeling something very different. (On occasions you do get uncanny resemblances to the other person. On one occasion the second person found themselves walking with just one arm swinging, exactly the same way the first person did.) The more possibilities you have to adapt your ankles, feet, hips, backs – in fact, everywhere – the more possible it is for you to really take on what you find and use it well. You have to go back to the Feldenkrais Method to help develop that!

A Wealth of Possibilities

There are many ways that Feldenkrais can enable an actor to find different uses of themselves for character.

Sometimes people come to me with difficult postural challenges that they want to explore for a character, and to look at how to avoid pain from playing that character for any length of time. One of the first times I used Feldenkrais, before I was even a fully trained practitioner, was to help an actress playing someone with severe kyphosis (hunchback). She needed to know how to find the way this person was and then how to go in and out of it, so that she could play believably and consistently but not get stuck in that posture all the time for all those months!

Then there are countless actors or students who have wanted to feel taller, more open, more upright, more balanced either to play a particular part, or just to have that possibility more generally available to them.

I also drew on Feldenkrais when working briefly on Alecky Blythe's verbatim play *Where Have I Been All My Life?* at the New Vic, Newcastle-under-Lyme, to enable some of the actors to find how to play characters from real life. I was given very specific descriptions of the characters, like 'a man in his sixties with a hip replacement that has gone wrong', or 'a man in his nineties who is blind and has emphysema', and to help one actor differentiate clearly between the two young men he was playing. In all these situations I got them to feel certain specific things they did naturally as themselves (e.g. feel what you do in your ribs when you walk) and then gave them a simple physical constraint (e.g. don't allow movement in your ribs on the right side as you walk). This changed what they did indirectly in a way that I knew would relate to the description (e.g. how they could use their right leg) without resorting to playing an idea of what they should look or be like (e.g. thinking about holding the leg). Sometimes we tried several different constraints till we found the right one. (See also discussion of the use of 'constraints' in Feldenkrais on pp. 196–9 and 226–7.)

Eventually, through Feldenkrais and what that enables you to see and explore, you will have experienced a wealth of possibilities that could emerge for a character without consciously thinking. Or, if you are devising work, you can see what some small shift in the detail of your self-use brings up. There are other very important aspects to explore: the rhythm of the person's movement, the way they take up space, and so on. Lecoq's teaching offers ways of exploring different qualities and ways of being through different elements and materials, and other methods can feed in here too: Laban, in particular, will give you another series of filters to play with – acceleration, direction, resistance/pressure and flow, for example, while Body Mind Centring gives you many different experiences of yourself in other ways. All of these combine well with Feldenkrais.

Allowing a Character to Emerge

Here is a game for you to explore what I mean by 'letting what is available come up'. I devised it before I was aware of Michael Chekhov's 'psychological gesture', but it turns out to be pretty close to it!

Moulding to a Character

This game can only draw on the possibilities you have available, but asks you to use the awareness and listening skills fostered by your Feldenkrais work to allow a character to emerge, rather than have you act out a preconceived idea. For this game you will need to have already done some research around your character so that you have a sense of their background, their social and personal history, and their journey in the play. But it also assumes that you have done very little practical work and not developed too many fixed ideas about how to play that character. You need to be very open to possibility, or you will just trot out your 'idea' regardless.

Begin standing simply and listen to how you are. Where is your weight in your feet? Do you stand on one leg more than the other? (Don't change it, just notice it.) Is there any sensation in your stomach or in your guts? What moves with your breath? How easy does it feel? Notice what places are working most in your legs, belly, back, shoulders, neck, jaw, face, fingers... and anything else that grabs your attention.

Now bring into your mind the character you have prepared. If the character has a big story arc, it may be that you will need to keep in mind what they want or who they are at a specific point in the play, and then do the exercise again at a different point. So now just bring them to mind.

Don't do anything consciously, but notice what changes in your sense of yourself. Maybe there are subtle shifts in the way you breathe, where your weight is, the level of work in certain places.

Let go of the character again and see what you do to 'return' to you. Sometimes what you undo is more noticeable than what you did.

Do this a few times for a few minutes each time and then let it go. Each time allow it to go further. Don't censor yourself because it doesn't fit your plan. If a load of rubbish happens you can chuck it out. It's just an exercise.

Gradually increase the sensation in the directions they are already going. Try not to interfere and turn it into something else. *Allow it to mould you, shape you, from within:* the way you stand and breathe and hold yourself.

See if you can allow movement to arrive as a consequence. It might feel right, it might not. Maybe moving around the space, maybe some kind of gesture or movement remaining where you are. You can let it get very big – unrealistically big if you like. You can also bring it back to very tiny, so that it is barely there, but is enough for you to feel the difference.

Try and bring it down to one repeated movement or one shape that somehow encapsulates this way of being.

Let it go slowly over a count of five or ten so you can feel what you undo.

Go back there and undo it again a few times so it is reversible. It will be there for you to re-find when you want, or you can decide it's not on the money and try something else. Anyway, it will all be useful information.

This kind of exercise can only draw on the possibilities you already have in you. For example, if you don't have any differentiation in how your foot meets the floor, if your weight always falls in the same pattern on your feet, if your ankle responds the same way, if the hip and the back can't adjust to allow the foot to land differently, then you will always plonk your foot down the same way when you walk, whatever character you bring to mind – or you might insist on making a difference that isn't fully integrated and, as a result, will look like a caricature. The more possibilities and the subtler the differences you have, the bigger and better the toolbox you have to draw on. Feldenkrais helps you develop that toolbox.

Creativity

At the heart of both clowning and Feldenkrais there is a beautiful mystery. In both, there is pleasure. There is delicacy. There is sensitivity and deep listening. I think this is why Dr Feldenkrais himself seems so like a clown to me. He is so fully present with himself, so authentically who he is and so alive to the people before him. And he has great clown hair.

Emily Davis, Feldenkrais for Artists in NYC[84]

Back to the Play Mat

In Part 1 we talked about how the organic learning a child does is playful, curious and explorative; how skills emerge over time, bit by bit, as they piece themselves together through trial and error. There is no known goal and no instructions about how to do it 'right'. Later in life there are games and sports that children play that have a containing pattern or rules within which they can explore, play, develop skills and make discoveries, be it 'witches and princesses' in the playground (where the rules are probably constantly being created and changed!); or painting, where the constraint might be that it is on paper with a brush; or riding a bike, where the constraint is having to keep moving on two wheels without falling off. All this learning is innately creative, and involves exploring and finding solutions within constraints. This is also how a Feldenkrais lesson works: it establishes constraints that enable us to become aware of what we have available, and to explore finding variations and differences.

> I think of play as training for the unexpected.
> Behavioural flexibility and variability is adaptive; in animals it's really important to be able to change your behaviour in a changing environment.
>
> *Marc Bekoff*[85]

That's why the Feldenkrais Method is so suitable for actors: because it encourages responsiveness, spontaneity, flexibility and adaptation to the situation – all great for survival, great for health in its broadest sense, and great for actors.

Not Knowing the End

Lie on your back, bring your knees up over your chest and hold your right knee with your right hand and left with left. Roll on to your right side like that and stay there, still holding your knees. Now, can you slide your left knee away from your head and down on to the floor below your right foot?

But the rules (or constraints) are:

- You must not let go of your knees or even slip your hand.

- You must keep a firm grip.

- Your face must follow your left knee – until the moment you discover it can do something else!

How do you get your knee to the floor below your right foot like that? What has to happen to the rest of you and where can you end up? There is a picture at the end of the chapter, but don't cheat by looking at it now. Just do the exercise! Try. Who cares if you don't work it out? If you do you will have the joy of discovery. If you don't, you will have the pleasure of being curious about the puzzle.

Not Knowing

Did you cheat? Congratulations if you didn't. You have to hang out with not knowing, and very few of us like doing that. We want to know where we are going. What we are 'meant' to be doing instead of just letting something happen and seeing where it goes. But this ability to let things happen without knowing where they will take you is what you need to create.

It is very clear in clowning because there the comedy of the situation is predicated on the clown not knowing what he/she is doing there at all. It is the awful comedy of it. 'You two are on stage and you have to play Othello. But you don't know the play. All you know is that it has something to do with a handkerchief.' That's one of the exercises I remember Gaulier setting us.

He would repeatedly take possibilities away from the performer who already had their plan of how to entertain us and be funny until they were so lost and 'in the shit' with no idea what to do, that the audience spontaneously started to laugh. Something real was happening at last.

If an actor carefully and diligently makes all their decisions about their character and how to play the scene, they leave no space for anything actually to happen. They get very busy in that corridor of theirs. At that point the audience switches off. Feldenkrais said it was the difference between 'exercise' and what he did. When you exercise you have an intended end. In his work you don't always know where you are going, or if you do you don't know the route. You try things out. See how it goes. Turn back, go another way. Allow it to turn up. Playing, rehearsing, without knowing exactly where you are going leaves room for something to turn up, something to surprise you – and the audience. *'Laissez le blague arriver,'* Philippe Gaulier used to say: 'Let the joke turn up.'

No Rules

This fits with what I said earlier about there not being fixed, universal rules about how to do things: nice known routes and certainties rather than this more risky venture into the unknown. It is difficult because we all like to be right and be successful, and we all like having a recipe that tells us what to do, and how and when to do it, but in terms of creativity it doesn't work. There may well be rules to a particular game, but nothing universal. Same in Feldenkrais: constraints within which to explore and relationships between places and patterns that work better or worse depending on what you want to do, but no fixed rules. Rules that need to be adhered to don't work for actors. If you always have to hold your head in one alignment, you are in trouble when you play a character who doesn't or when you do something that involves moving it out of that alignment (it's all in Part 2b on posture). Constraints or rules of the game are great for creativity because they involve problem-solving, variety and thinking on your feet. Universal rules of how you always ought to do something are not because they don't. Not to make a rule out of it...!

Not Forcing

Not forcing means allowing, but it also means having the delicacy and the sensitivity to let something grow from very little, to let it breathe and play and develop into something. That is an exciting thing to watch happen between people. When an actor comes on, ignores what the other actor offers and forces an idea through or forces their emotions and intentions on us, we tend to turn off. It becomes boring or even unpleasant to watch. It feels dead. Nothing is really happening. Sometimes it can feel like an assault.

If the Feldenkrais Method does anything, it teaches you sensitivity: sensitivity to fine differences between this little movement and that; the way this variation feels and that; between pushing and inviting, doing and allowing, too little and too much, easy and not-quite-so easy. It gives you a sense of where the edges are and what it means to go beyond them. It shows you how little you need to do to make a huge difference: change the way you move your eyes or hold your jaw, and your head rolls utterly differently; feel where your weight needs to be for your leg to lift and become weightless.

Push and strain and work and that's all you get. Who wants to watch that? It gets in the way of everything. In particular, it gets in the way of listening, and listening is what acting is all about. In a sense, 'actor' is a terrible name as it just implies doing. Maybe we should say 'listeners' or 'responders' instead. Feldenkrais trains you to quieten yourself down and listen. It may be that you work in a form that invites you to push beyond boundaries or uses tension as part of its creative style, but there is a difference between that and having limiting habits restricting where your boundaries are in the first place, or compulsive tension that is not an expressive choice.

Limitations

As John Wright puts it on p. vii, the Method can widen your sense of yourself and what you can do. Sometimes it throws you up against your habitual limitations, which you may not have known you had, and that can be very hard. But just as often it can show you a way through that you had no idea was there and in the gentlest way possible. I have had clients in tears discovering that they don't have to be stuck in the way they thought they always would be or didn't even know they were. Tears of sadness that they didn't find out earlier and tears of relief that they have found a way out now. It's true for actors too. 'But I always thought I was clumsy,' said one student actor to me as he discovered he could spiral up from the floor effortlessly and gracefully. His face was a picture of amazement and delight. It had taken just an hour to suggest he could change his whole idea of himself. The implications of that are huge for his creative potential as an actor.

Pleasure

> To make the impossible possible, the possible easy and the easy pleasurable.

> *Moshe Feldenkrais*

As Dick McCaw, Director of the International Workshop Festival for many years, said to me, you need to strip the anxiety out of learning and put the pleasure in as much as possible or not much happens (see also Part 6 on anxiety). It's true for creating too, which can become pressured, tense and stunted otherwise. Okay, stress, exhaustion and even bitter arguments can have their place in creativity, but my experience is that they are not conducive except under special circumstances involving very particular groups of people. They usually lead to people retreating inwards, not daring to risk – with fairly unwatchable results.

Less anxiety and more pleasure is fostered by the Feldenkrais Method, where there are no gold stars for being 'correct' and no minus points for not 'achieving'. Most of the time you are lying on the floor not having to deal with what anyone else is doing, and therefore not comparing yourself to how 'well' they are doing it. You go at your own pace, and as long as you get curious about what you are doing and really involved in exploring, you will come out with discoveries and new abilities – all of which is usually very pleasurable.

'*Amusez-vous merde!*' ('Enjoy yourself, for fuck's sake!') Philippe Gaulier used to shout on occasions at some poor student riddled with anxiety or trying desperately to 'get it right': maybe not the best way to reduce anxiety and get someone to enjoy themselves, but his frustration was sometimes understandable and his philosophy impeachable. His highest praise for a clown in my day was: '*Comme elle est conne!*' ('She is a complete idiot!') What other teacher used to berate his students similarly, if a little more gently, with the words: 'Don't you know how to be silly? Why is it that no one in this room can be silly?'

Ah yes. That would be Dr Moshe Feldenkrais.

Part 5

Voice and Breath

5. Voice and Breath

I don't think I need to spend much time explaining why it's important for an actor to be able to use their voice! If you ask a new drama student why they need vocal training, they will probably come up with the need to 'project' for theatre and to work on their singing. A resonant, strain-free and versatile speaking voice is going to be an important tool for any kind of acting, screen as well as stage. A voice that is not facilitated well by the breath, cannot make use of natural resonance and is 'strangled' (forced by tension or overwork) won't have as much range in terms of volume as will a trained voice, but it is also, more significantly, unlikely to have as much range of expression, conviction and connection to feeling. In my public practice, I sometimes meet people who cannot express the depth and wealth of opinion they have in a way that enables them to be heard and valued. It is almost as if their voice is being cut off or diminished, and with it their words too. Feldenkrais himself suffered from laryngitis aged twelve, and even at that tender age worked out that there was nothing 'wrong' with him, but that he was developing tensions and difficulties in his own musculature which he could improve himself. Mark Reese, his biographer, says: 'He understood that those muscular contractions reflected a conflict between his desire to express himself and his fear of disapproval.'[86] I was talking to an experienced voice teacher recently about the need for an actor to 'find their voice' to be able to inhabit the character convincingly, but she stressed that it can be the other way around too: the ability to inhabit the character convincingly is often what is needed to find and release the actor's voice for the role. Already we are in a wider territory than vocal training in terms of what 'finding your voice' might involve.

I have the pleasure of working in drama schools in which I can talk to voice teachers who have a great understanding of the delicate and detailed movement of the cartilages of the larynx, the soft palate and tongue, in specific ways to enable different kinds of sound for singing as well as speaking. Feldenkrais included some but not all of this in his lessons as we have them, but we can take recent anatomical and physiological understanding and create Awareness Through Movement lessons from it. There are Feldenkrais teachers who are also Voice Craft or Estill teachers who have that knowledge and do exactly that – most notably Maggy Burrowes in the UK and Robert Sussuma in the US. There are also Feldenkrais teachers whose experience and learning enable them to take Feldenkrais lessons further into voice, such as Richard Corbeil in the US.[87] There are vocal systems like Kristin Linklater's that are, conversely, very influenced by Feldenkrais and which the Method is often used to support. These approaches are good and exciting, and I would recommend them highly.

Because of a wider awareness of what can affect the voice, Feldenkrais teachers who are not specifically vocal coaches can teach a great deal to enable voice too. Indeed, the Method is increasingly used to support voice training as well as movement at drama schools. The head of voice at one London school once told me that since they had had Feldenkrais classes in the school, her teaching had been able to 'sink in like butter'. In the Peter Brook/Teatro El Campesino workshop I described right at the start of the book, Dr Feldenkrais spent almost half the time on lessons for voice. In my private practice I regularly work with voice teachers, singers, actors and those who have issues with their breath and voice.

Feldenkrais for Voice

It is arguable that almost any Feldenkrais lesson you do is likely to enable your voice in some way. And that's because your voice is not a separate thing from the rest of you. This idea – that the voice might have something to do with movement – is not on many laypeople's radars, and students are often surprised to find themselves doing so many physical exercises in their voice lessons. You don't have to think about it for long to get the point. After all, the muscles involved in breathing are also involved in moving: improve the one and you enable the other. Any of the parts of ourselves that we habitually hold, tighten, compress or simply leave out of the picture may also be places we need to use in different ways for the breath and to make sound. Then there are also specific lessons in the Method that enable the breath or develop awareness of the tongue, jaw, palate and the whole inside of the head cavity (which includes the main areas of resonance). These lessons are, as is all of the Method, exploratory in their nature, ensuring you bring your attention to the different places involved, inviting you to begin to use those places in a greater variety of ways so as to enhance vocal production. They don't give you a 'to-do' list for specific sounds as much as they lower the level of unnecessary tension, create more choice, invite you to feel the connections between voice, breath and how you use your whole self; and enable you to let go of some of the compulsive habits that are getting in the way of better breathing, greater resonance or improved clarity.

For example, we have strong, often very old, habits around how we hold the jaw and tongue. You might notice them especially when you are concentrating, writing, doing something difficult or feeling strong emotions. Think of the child that sticks their tongue out when writing, or notice what you do yourself with your mouth when you are working out a difficult maths problem, or playing a tricky passage on a musical instrument – or perhaps the feeling you have in the jaw, mouth and throat when you are sad, angry or anxious. What you do with your jaw and tongue is also related to your neck, and given your neck is part of your spine, what happens there doesn't only involve the movement of the head but has an effect on the whole of the spine, with consequences for every movement you make – and vice versa. If you want to feel the connection of the jaw and tongue to the neck try this (I have included a little bit about the eyes too, as they are also part of this interesting picture):

Head, Jaw, Tongue – and Eyes!

Lie on your back with your knees bent, feet planted, and feel where your head rests. Which part of the back of the head touches the floor? Where is Home?

Roll your head left and right gently and see what movement you have easily. Be sure to really listen to what is truly easy and stop at the first moment you feel an interference, so you will notice if anything changes in this range of real ease.

Put your tongue out of the right corner of your mouth and very gently let it lead your head to right a few times. How does it go? Is it different? Then the same to the left. Now turn the head again on its own and feel the difference.

This time, move your tongue to the right and try and take your head to left. If your tongue is really going to the right it will hardly be possible! But be gentle!

Roll your head on its own again and feel how it is.

This time open your mouth a tiny bit. Move your jaw a teeny bit left and right – very soft and small and slow as you can easily do too much here. Just enough that your two front teeth, top and bottom, go a little bit out of alignment. It may be easier one way than the other. Listen to back of neck – you may feel something shift there at base of skull in tonus of muscles.

Now move your jaw to right and turn your head to right. Jaw to left and head to left. Listen to your eyes as well. Do they go with head or jaw or neither?

Move your jaw and eyes and head to right and left all together.

Move your jaw and eyes to right but this time try and take your head to the left. Now jaw and eyes to right and try and move your head to left. Finally, move them left and right all together again.

Now simply turn your head on its own and notice the range of real ease.

Feel where your head rests too. Where is Home now? You can do this sitting as well as lying down.

It would take a lot of pages to give you a game or lesson for each of the following, so you will have to take it on trust that using your shoulders and arms independently of your head (and vice versa) and in synergy with the ribs has consequences for your breath and throat – and how your feet, legs and pelvis support and enable your posture and movement makes a big difference to the freedom of your whole structure, as well as your breath and voice. I hope that you are getting the point that every time you strain excessively somewhere to produce a movement, you are likely to feel it in your breathing pattern and hear it in your voice. You can feel it if you try to speak while you are lifting something heavy or are doing intense exercise, but here is something more subtle to try:

Voice and Movement

Walk around the room. Every now and again sit down, and then get up and walk on.

At the same time as you do this, make an 'aaaah' sound, and notice when your voice is interrupted or strained by the effort of getting down or getting up.

Now go back to *Lesson 8: Getting Up and Down from the Floor with a Twist* on p. 145.

Make the movement as smooth as you can and now add the 'aaah' sounds again. Are you able to make the sound without as much interruption or change in quality of the sound? Notice the parts of the movement where your voice is not so easy. Don't try to control your voice, but see if you can change the quality of the movement at these points and notice if your voice is less strained or strangled.

If you found a difference you might be able to appreciate that many of the issues for voice are the same as for movement of any kind – inappropriate levels and distribution of work through the system; substituting muscular effort for support from the skeleton and ground; patterns of holding and tension; lack of clarity in the pattern of movement. It is therefore true that any Feldenkrais lesson is likely to have an effect on the breath and voice too, because any lesson works with these issues. If you do specific voice lessons, the voice teacher's concerns will also include whether you are substituting force for skilful and appropriate use of the breath and vocal apparatus, and whether that is enabled by the rest of you. Skill rather than effort. Same old, same old. As one singing teacher said to me, you may be able to sound good in one song, but if the technique is poor and if you are substituting effort for good use, it won't hold up over time or through a range of songs.

As with all of the Feldenkrais Method, one book cannot possibly give you the whole picture – and certainly not one chapter when it comes to voice – so if you are interested it is worth look-ing at the practitioners I mentioned earlier too. For now let's take some of the more specific aspects individually to give you a sense of how it works. And you will find we have covered some of them already!

Posture/Acture

At the risk of repeating myself: if the skeleton is not able to do its job of supporting you sufficiently because it is being pulled a little this way or that, then muscles that are not well suited to the job will have to start joining in and working to hold you up – and some of that extraneous work is likely to interfere with your breath and your voice, as we saw in *Lesson 6: Lifting the Head*. The job of your 'posture' is to maintain a good enough balance to allow you to do what you want and not get in the way: for all of that I refer you back Part 2.

It is all too easy for the idea that posture is dynamic and is about relationships of different parts of you in movement to go out the window at this point, for it all to become about standing up 'straight' in a specific 'alignment' in order to facilitate the voice. Specific positions may be important to enable certain vocal exercises, but if that is interpreted as a model for how to be *all the time*, then what happens when you are giving your dying speech in *Antony and Cleopatra*? Are you standing up straight or lying neatly in a straight line then? What happens when you play a slouchy teenager or a broken-down old woman, or you have to sing or talk upside down? I have said it already: posture has to be about finding support from the skeleton and from the ground in all kinds of positions and movements. It is important for an actor (indeed for anyone) to explore and understand the relationship between their voice, breath and posture, but not to become reliant on one organisation or one specific 'alignment' only.

So we are thrown back to the idea of relationships between parts as fundamental to the notion of posture (or acture). Having a sense of the relationship of the torso and pelvis to the head is obviously key here, so that the comparatively little muscles of the neck and throat are not trying to do work that the torso and pelvis can do. *Lesson 6* showed this well: lift the head just with the neck and you compress the throat and strain the voice. Allow the chest to bend, the back to lengthen and the pelvis to curl up so the big muscles do the donkey work of lifting the head, helped by the support from the ground and the C-shape of the spine. Then you will find the neck is freed of the work so it can move, and the throat is no longer compressed so you can speak – and if the ground and the C-shape do enough of the work, then a better use of the abdominal muscles can allow your breathing to be easier into the bargain.

Balance of the Head

It is particularly worth noting that the skull is carefully balanced at a point where there is a little more weight in front of the spine than behind, so the muscles of the back of the neck do more to hold the head up than the muscles at the front, which gives the throat some freedom. If the pattern of posture means that the skull's weight falls too much in front of the spine, the muscles of the back of the neck will have to do even more to keep the head upright, and that in turn may demand that the anchoring muscles around the neck towards the front, and even the delicate little muscles attaching at the hyoid bone in the throat, may work to counterbalance the increasing pull from the neck. In this picture, the head, throat and the jaw will not be as free as they could be to facilitate movement or voice. This is just one rather oversimplified scenario, but it gives you an idea of the delicacy of balance required between the muscles. It is not possible to correct this kind of thing muscle by muscle, as there is a great web from the tiny muscles at the base of the skull and jaw, to the strong and very visible V of the sternocleidomastoid muscles, which run down each side of the front of the throat to the huge trapezius muscle at the back, which in turn runs from halfway down the back out to the shoulders and up to the base of the skull – as well as many more to the ribs and shoulders and down the front and back of the cervical spine or neck. What is required is a delicate balance through the whole structure, which only the nervous system below the level of conscious instruction can really regulate. This is why the Feldenkrais approach of noticing and playing with the changing relationships between parts in a structured way, out of which an effective functional balance can emerge as Home, is so helpful.

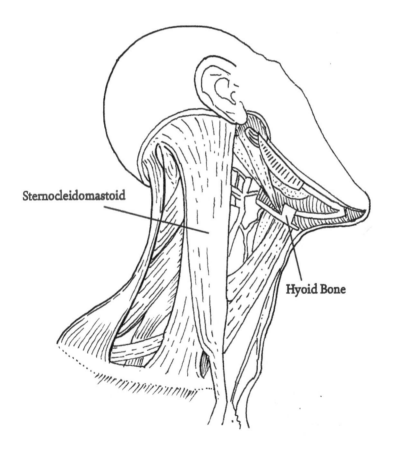

Sternocleidomastoid

Hyoid Bone

The Seventh Cervical

It always sounds like the title of a sci-fi film, but actually the seventh cervical is the bottom vertebra of the neck, which meets the top vertebra of the spine (first thoracic). It forms the vital gateway between the neck and the back, a junction that is also influenced by the rest of the spine below it, the shoulderblades to either side, and the junction of the collarbones and breastbone in front.

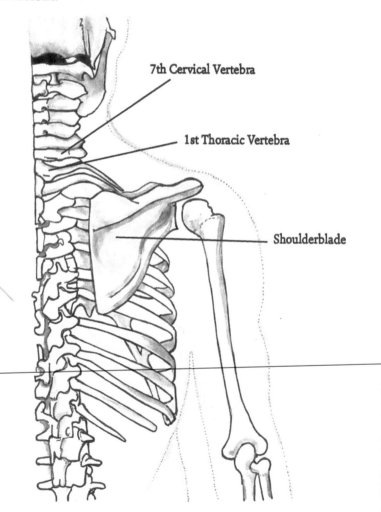

7th Cervical Vertebra

1st Thoracic Vertebra

Shoulderblade

One typical example I can give you of its importance: a student comes to see me who has been told that he pushes his chin too far forward so that the back of his neck is shortened and the front of the neck is pulled tight. As the delicate balance of the skull is out, all sorts of muscles are also working harder than they should to stop the head falling forward. Sometimes students like this will have been told to lengthen the back of their neck and pull their chin in and down: not bad advice, except they usually can't lengthen the back of their neck, and they find pulling the chin in simply compresses their throat and makes everything worse. Often their pattern goes with a sunken chest, which they also try to push forward, compounding the problem by compressing the throat more and gluing the collarbones to the ribs. What often gets overlooked here, or is just hard to facilitate, is that the seventh cervical and first thoracic are usually stuck in a position that pushes the base of the neck forward and narrows the space at the very top of the back between the shoulderblades. If these vertebrae don't unstick and find their mobility, the very top of the back cannot widen to let the neck find its length. Still with me? It's not easy to picture unless you have felt it. Let's have a go.

Pecking and Chicken Wings

Either sitting or standing, move your head directly forward, keeping it parallel with the floor and without tipping it up or down. Your chin goes straight forward, neither lifting nor dropping: like a chicken pecking. Feel what happens in your chest. Does it lift or sink? Now bring your chin straight in towards your neck without lifting or dropping. Feel what happens in your chest. Don't do anything special, just feel the difference. Also listen to the very top of your back. Does anything happen there? Is there any forward or backward movement, widening or narrowing in that place?

Now bend your arms and take your elbows backwards at the same time as your head slides forward. Once again, feel what happens in your chest but also in the top of your back between your shoulderblades: do you feel the potential for narrowing between the blades now?

Then as you take the head back, move your elbows out to side and forward like a chicken flapping its wings. Feel where the base of your neck can slide back into the widening space between your shoulderblades as the elbows go forward, so the chin can also come back comfortably without compressing your throat.

Now make movements smaller and smaller in each direction till you find the middle.

There are actually whole ATM lessons around this theme, and this game is just to give you a little sense of it. Sometimes the seventh cervical and adjacent vertebrae are really too stuck or it is too difficult for the person to feel and differentiate any movements in this unusual place. In this case, a Feldenkrais practitioner can work with their hands to facilitate the movement of these verte-brae as part of a whole hands-on lesson (see Functional Integration in Part 6) – but it is completely worth exploring as the difference can be really radical. My students are often shocked at the new feeling of where their head can sit, and how their chest can now open more easily – as well as the release of their diaphragm, which is no longer being squashed by the sinking of their lower ribcage, and the new freedom in the front of their neck/throat. Oh and their lovely new height or long neck as well!

Breath

All the above applies to breath, but it is worth spending time specifically on the parts of the body that are involved in breathing. There is not just one way to breathe: how you breathe when you run is different from when you are reading this book or when you lift a heavy weight; when you are frightened you breathe differently from when you are happy; and you do something very interesting with your breath and breathing apparatus when you laugh or cry or sneeze. Some ways of breathing excite or stimulate, and some are calming. And then there may be specific ways you learn to breathe for specific activities. Have a look at Morio Higaonna Sensei doing Sanchin Kata (youtu.be/kybxNOlnl20) and you will see a very extraordinary (and very difficult) use of breath for power. Yoga has different ways of breathing to suit a number of different purposes. Brass and wind instrument players, swimmers, singers (to name a few), may learn specific organisations of the breath to suit the specific demands of that activity. The fact that they are all different does not make one correct and the others wrong – they are just specific for a particular purpose. I often have students who are confused by the plethora of different advice about breathing, but the answer is to look at what the giver of advice is seeking to enable. The differences may simply be that what they are aiming at is different. In the variety of activities in everyday life, your breath will change spontaneously in response to your greater or lesser need for oxygen, unless something gets in the way of it – either because you feel you should 'correct' it or simply because some options are not sufficiently available.

As Kristin Linklater stresses, an actor needs a voice that is above all responsive, and responsiveness, as we have seen, means not being too fixed in one way of doing anything. That includes breathing, since emotional fluctuations, as well as varying levels and intensity of activity, require adaptation of the breath. With the Feldenkrais Method we can help make more options available for your system to draw on spontaneously, as needed, without conscious thinking. Then you can learn to differentiate more easily between specialised ways of breathing for specific activities (like singing or fighting). In addition, you may be dealing with nerves, so some ways of loosening the constrictions anxiety causes and using the breath to calm the system are helpful too (but we will look at that in Part 6). There are many breathing lessons in the Method; the one I have chosen for you here covers a lot of ground and is very unusual, so it is a good one to try as a taster.

A distinction is often made between abdominal (belly) and thoracic (chest) breathing. In real life we tend to use a mixture. In some ways this is a strange distinction, as your lungs are always in your chest and they have to fill and empty. You never actually breathe into your belly: it's full of guts and other organs! In so-called abdominal breathing we rely more on the big muscle of the diaphragm flattening down as it contracts, pulling and opening the lungs downwards, and on the lower ribs opening, and a bit less on the upper ribs opening and lifting. It feels like breathing into the belly because of the expansion downwards, which means the abdomen is forced to swell. In thoracic breathing, while the diaphragm still descends, more room is made higher in the lungs by means of a greater amount of lifting and opening of the ribs via the intercostal muscles.

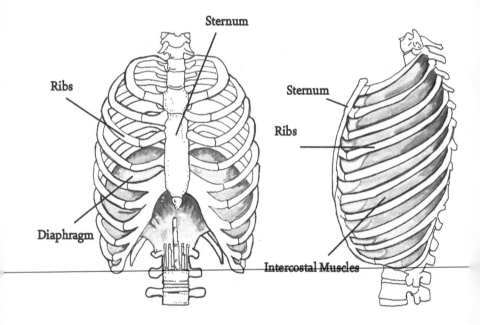

This lesson explores all of it. I always have to remind my students that this lesson is not about *how* to breathe. It simply makes every part more available, whatever your needs.

Lesson 11: See-Saw Breathing

Start by trying out your voice. Make some long notes on an 'aah' at whatever pitch is comfortable (try a few), and then also just speak. Notice the resonance, the volume, the quality of the sound, the pitch of your speaking voice.

Lie on your back with long legs and just notice which parts of your back rest on the floor clearly.

Bend your knees and plant your feet. Notice what moves most when you breathe. Do you feel it more in your belly? If so, how low do you feel movement? As far as the groin? Do you only feel it in the front? Do you feel anything in your lower back or sides of the waist? Maybe you feel it more in the ribs – or as well. If so, what parts of the ribs? Just the lower ones or the higher ones too? The top rib runs right under the collarbone! What about the sides of your chest or back?

For a few breaths, focus on your abdomen, i.e. below the waist: your belly and lower back. When you breathe in, imagine you are blowing up a balloon inside you, and as you breathe out it deflates. Don't be in a hurry to drag in another breath. Breathe all the way out and wait for the new breath to come. Although you may take in a little more than your usual breath, don't force anything.

Notice if your lower back moves on the floor and at what point in the cycle of the breath. Does the pelvis rock? Breathe only into the front of the belly so it gets big. As we know, it's not really breathing into your belly because you have no lungs in your belly. It is the diaphragm lowering that lessens the space for the organs in this area so the abdomen presses out to make more space. This movement at the front is likely to hollow your lower back a bit and rock the pelvis towards the tailbone. This balloon is not a perfect sphere if you think about it, it is just the front of it. You have the bones of the pelvis and the spine at the back so it can't expand backwards in the same way, but there is still some space there, especially in the area of the bottom floating ribs and waist – and your spine can move, so the image of expanding at the back and sides gives you something rather different.

Now see if when you breathe in, you can also expand the back of the waist, so your lower back moves or glues to the floor a little more on the in-breath and the pelvis stays quieter. Put your hands on the sides of your waist near the floor, and as you breathe in you should feel it bulge out a little there into your hands. You will feel pressure on the pelvic floor, so if you have any issues with it (e.g. following childbirth), go gently. Do not force it powerfully.

When you have found this see if you can find the same movement without an in-breath. Can you just find the muscles that can make it expand like that?

Now direct the breath into the chest instead. Pull in the waist and blow up the chest like Superman. But don't force it. See if you can allow the ribs to lift and open all around the chest-sides and back as well as front and, if there is any availability, right up to the collarbones. Breathe all the way out and let it sink. This kind of breathing is sometimes known as 'costal breathing' (*'costa'* is the latin name for 'rib') because it makes full use of the ribs and not just the diaphragm. In our daily life we use a mix of diaphragmatic and costal breathing, but specialist activities can require one more than the other, or even one exclusively.

Try this version without breathing in. See if you can find the muscles that pull the chest open like this.

Now pull in the belly and take a breath into the chest so it expands as just now, but this time when you breathe out have the sense that you push it out through the abdomen and pelvic floor – so that the abdomen expands and the chest sinks. And again, many times. This is called paradoxical or inverse-abdominal breathing, as it is opposite to what we normally do. As you do it you may begin to feel that there is a sort of a see-saw starting to happen between the belly and chest, one expands and the other sinks, and then vice versa.

Now take a breath into the chest again with the belly pulled in, but this time hold the breath and make the action of paradoxical breathing with the muscles only: so sink the chest and expand the belly. *Then keep holding the breath but reverse it again: pull in the belly and expand the chest. Keep alternating.* Do it as many times as the breath allows, and then take a pause and have another go on another breath. It may feel a little like squeezing a hot-water bottle at the top so the water is pushed into the bottom, and then squeezing it at the bottom so the water is pushed up into the top. Go softly, slowly and gently, allowing the transition to be smooth and easy. Notice if your back can stay on the floor, in which case you are using the whole of the diaphragm not just the front part.

Once you get the movement clearly and easily, you can play with making it small, light and quick, as well as big and slow.

Let your legs down and feel any differences in the parts of your back that lie on the floor.

Stand up and try out you voice again as you did at the start. Notice any differences in the resonance, the volume, the quality of the sound – and the pitch of your speaking voice.

Even standing might well feel different. If you think about how many parts of your torso were involved in that movement, it would not be surprising that your standing could have changed. It is actually a great 'core' lesson too!

Jaw, Tongue, Mouth

Another big subject, and there are many lessons available for this. Many of us clamp the jaw, grind the teeth, have tension in the root of the tongue or a tendency to close the throat. And all of us have simple habits as to how we use these structures that we can explore. There are a number of lessons that work with the delicate movements of the jaw, and there are some good Feldenkrais CDs available described as being for TMJ (temporomandibular joint) syndrome that are actually great for anyone. (The temporomandibular joint is where the jaw meets the skull. You can find it if you almost stick your fingers in your ears, but feel just in front of the ear there instead. See picture opposite.)

We saw in the little game earlier how the jaw, tongue, neck and eyes are interrelated, but here is one of my favourite lessons that hits a number of spots all at the same time, it is a simplified version of 'Palate, Mouth and Teeth' (no. 23 in the Alexander Yanai series). If you do have TMJ syndrome, please take it very slowly and only where it feels comfortable to go. In anything you do with the tongue and jaw you must go gently, slowly and softly. The TM joint is very delicate, and for some people it is very easily strained. The muscles of the jaw are very powerful and trying to use any force at all is likely to create strong resistance and more tension. You may also be shocked to see just how big your tongue is and how far back the root goes. It goes some way to explaining its effect on your throat, jaw and neck.

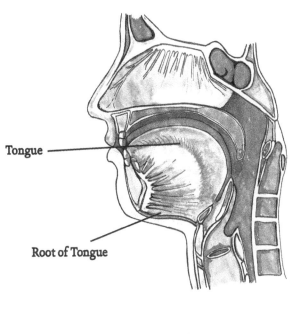

Tongue

Root of Tongue

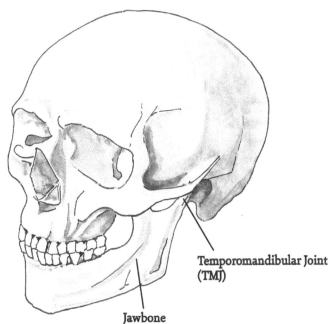

Temporomandibular Joint
(TMJ)

Jawbone

Lesson 12: Painting Your Mouth

Start by trying out your voice. Make some long notes on an 'aaah' at whatever pitch is comfortable (try a few), and then also just speak. Notice the resonance, the volume, the quality of the sound, the pitch of your speaking voice.

Lie on your back with your feet planted.

Slowly explore the shape of the right side of the roof of your mouth with your tongue. (Do all this lesson on the right side of the mouth only first.) Notice the shape of the roof of your mouth on this side – all the funny ridges and curves of your hard palate. You won't get as far back as the soft palate but you might feel how the sensation changes as you get close. Don't force it where it doesn't want to go.

Imagine your tongue is a paintbrush. Starting in the middle, slowly begin to paint the roof of your mouth on the right, in stripes from front to back.

Paint it again cross-wise this time, from the middle out to the right and back, also in stripes. Only to the right. Still slowly.

Now, still on the right side only, paint the floor of your mouth with your tongue. Paint it in stripes again front to back, curling the tip of back towards its root. Feel the shape of the floor of your mouth on the right.

Paint it again cross-wise from the middle to the right and back. Slowly.

Place your tongue behind the top front teeth. Slowly paint the back of each tooth with it in some colour you like, travelling only to the right from the middle and back to the middle. Feel each tooth and paint it well. If it is at all uncomfortable to get to the back teeth, go only as far as is comfortable and see if you can picture these back teeth instead, as if you were painting them.

Do the same with the back of the bottom teeth again travelling from the middle to the right only and back again. Go slowly and carefully, only as far as is comfortable.

Do the same with the front of the top teeth, placing your tongue on the front of the tooth but inside the lip – again from the middle to the right. It is a little more demanding on the jaw to have the tongue in this place so go only as far as is comfortable.

Now paint the front of the bottom teeth. From the middle to the right only.

Place the tongue inside the right cheek and paint as much of the inside of the cheek as you can manage comfortably, easily and slowly. If the jaw or tongue feels too stretched or forced you are going too far or doing too much – be gentle.

Place your tongue on the back of the top row of front teeth. Run it all round the back of the front teeth and continue round the back of the lower teeth as well (as far as is comfortable), making a half-circumference of the mouth like this. Then back again, round to the right of the bottom teeth and up to the top teeth and back to the middle.

Do the same with the tongue on the outside of the teeth. Just on the right.

Now you have painted the whole of the right side of your mouth with the tongue, how does it feel? Is it bigger or smaller than the left side? Do other parts of your face or throat feel different? Is there more of a sense of space in the right TM joint?

Do all of this on the left.

Stand up and notice how you feel in standing and whether the way you carry your head or anything else feels a little different. Now try out your voice again. Make some long notes on an 'aaah' and then also just speak. Notice the resonance, the volume, the quality of the sound, the pitch of your speaking voice.

Voice Games with Constraints

A lot of the Feldenkrais Method uses constraints. In a sense, every time the teacher gives an instruction they set constraints. 'Bring your arm forward' rules out taking the arm up, down, behind or some other direction: it constrains you to one direction. Feldenkrais lessons typically go much further than that, creating constraints so that you have to find movement in a place you might otherwise avoid. For example: 'Lie on your back, bring your arms directly above you, put the palms together and then take the arms to the left.' In response to this, many people will simply bend the left elbow or let the right hand slide up the inside of the left arm. In this way not much happens that enables the movement of the shoulderblade or allows the person to feel how the movement of their arms is connected to the ribs and spine. So the lesson asks for two constraints: the palms mustn't slide on each other and the left elbow mustn't bend. That way you have to start to lift and slide the right shoulder and eventually do something with the ribs and the whole back that might travel right down to the pelvis.

There are a number of simple games with constraints you can play with for voice that invite you to use more of your vocal apparatus more effectively. In the discussion at the end of the workshop for Peter Brook's company and Teatro El Campesino, Feldenkrais says that he feels the improvements one actor is making in his voice have slowed down a great deal since an initial burst of improvement. He suggests that this actor practices a speech absolutely as if speaking but making no noise. He says the actor will make another leap of improvement like that. His point is partly that doing the same exercises over and over begins to produce fewer results as we get into a habit of how we do the lesson: the nervous system becomes habituated to the same sensations in doing it rather than being interested in the new sensation it originally produced, and so we learn progressively less. When you make no sound, though, you get a very novel and different experience of speaking: without sound you are thrown on to the sensations of what you are doing with the various parts of your vocal apparatus in a different way. Try it.

There are a variety of different possibilities in this game to emphasise different aspects of making sound.

Constraints for Voice

Think of a short nursery rhyme, or a few lines of a poem or speech you know really well (so you don't have to think about remembering words).

Say it normally first and notice how clear it is and what you can tell about the different parts of your mouth you are using. Then:

Keep your teeth fixed together but allow the tongue, lips and inside of the mouth to do whatever is needed to say it as clearly as possible. Just don't let the teeth separate. Feel how your tongue and lips have to help out with this constraint. Say it many times like this. Now say it normally and notice the difference in how you use your lips and tongue and in the clarity of your speech.

Now keep the lips together but let the teeth, tongue and inside of the mouth do whatever is needed to say it as well as you can. The lips never separate. Many times. Notice how the inside of your mouth changes shape, what the soft palate (roof of the mouth towards the back) and the base of your mouth/root of the tongue do to help. You might feel other places very active too. Now speak the lines again allowing the lips to move again.

Now let the tongue hang out of your mouth and speak the lines many times without letting the tongue back in. Make the diction as good as you can make it under this constraint. Then speak again.

I hope this is enough to give you a clearer idea of how the Feldenkrais Method supports voice training and enables you to explore in a different way. If this area is of particular interest to you, I recommend strongly that you go further and look into the work of some of the other teachers I have mentioned (see the Appendix).

Part 6

Injury and Anxiety

6. Injury and Anxiety

Injury

It is important to remember that Feldenkrais is not a medical practice. Its arena is educational. When it comes to injury and other conditions, a form of re-education can often play a crucial role. So it is that actors, just like everyone else, frequently first discover the Feldenkrais Method because they have an injury that has already had medical attention but needs something more, or they have a pain that has become chronic and that nothing seems to shift. Injury and pain for actors can be disastrous. I know this only too well as it happened to me: it's not a bad example to look at to see what Feldenkrais can do.

I had drifted away from Feldenkrais as I was touring or in rep out of London and couldn't get to any class regularly. It was true that studying with Monika Pagneux and then taking classes at The Open Centre in Old Street for a while had had a transformative effect on my sense of self, as well as my movement, and that the things I had learnt had stuck, but I know now that I had hardly begun. It stood me in pretty good stead even so. In my early thirties I had an accident and tore the cartilage in my right knee. It went misdiagnosed and pretty much dismissed by my doctor and by the first physiotherapist I saw. Then, despite finding another physiotherapist who did some very good work, it still didn't feel safe or stable. It wasn't until six months later when I tore it further just reaching for something while sitting on the ground at a picnic, that the doctor agreed it was more than a strain and suggested I needed an operation. During this time I had been going for auditions leaning on a stick, knowing it was unlikely I could accept the job anyway. Not a great way to go for a meeting with Mike Leigh, for example, as I did. It was pretty distressing and did my career no good at all, so I agreed to the operation. Afterwards I headed back into Feldenkrais. While not being able to walk had rekindled my interest in it, I was actually thinking more about doing the training than hopeful of help with my knee – my understanding of Feldenkrais was from the perspective of developing skill, so I didn't realise that it was exactly what I needed now.

The operation was done very well by a very good surgeon who specialises in knees. I needed it because there was a piece of meniscus (cartilage) torn loose and flapping about in there. The physiotherapy was also very good in keeping the musculature active so that it didn't waste when I couldn't really use it. And yet all was not right. I still didn't use my right leg fully, and it didn't feel as strong or reliable. It was hard to keep the muscles from wasting without constant exercise, and sometimes I would still get pain. It was only after I got stuck into Feldenkrais again that it dawned on me that this had been an accident waiting to happen, because of the way my back habitually twisted and bent, and how that related to my leg and made it vulnerable. Quite suddenly after a hands-on lesson (see Functional Integration below) – no doubt also prepared for by many Awareness Through Movement classes – I stood up *on* my injured right leg properly and realised I had not felt that for years. If ever, perhaps. The way I could feel my pelvis over my leg with the weight really *on* the leg felt totally new, but I could not have told you that it had been missing before. My leg suddenly felt so strong and clear and supportive – nothing like the slightly dodgy, weakened one I had thought I was saddled with for life. No amount of strengthening exercises had enabled me to feel that kind of support from my leg, and now I had simply got up from a table and there it was. I was shocked. As Feldenkrais trainer (and athlete and aikidoist) Jeff Haller, says:

> Our muscle tone is turned on by our relationship to the environment. That means the very specific ways we find support from the surfaces we are on. Moshe spoke clearly about how it is that we continually find support as the basis for action. The more specific, more refined, more clear you are in the way you find where you are supporting yourself from, the more clear any action you make will be.[88]

That's what had happened for me, and it meant that my musculature now stabilised almost immediately. Rapidly now, bits of movement that I had lost around the edges without noticing came back. With no pain. I could leap up from sitting without using my hands, run properly without hesitation and cartwheel again. I remember coming home from training and rushing about with my baby daughter for the sheer pleasure of moving like that again. I really hadn't noticed I had stopped doing those kind of things until it all started flooding back – or perhaps I had just accepted its disappearance as getting older and had begun to define myself as a person 'with a bad knee'.

It did take some time working with the Method to feel with confidence that I was no longer a person with a bad knee. In finding new layers of sensitivity and awareness, I began to notice the movement patterns that triggered the pain. I found different ways of using my whole self, of finding support from the skeleton and the ground that enabled me to feel the support of the leg better. I started to recognise when I was beginning to fall back into old pain-associated ways of moving. I used Feldenkrais lessons to make a clear shift in my whole self-use and head off trouble earlier and earlier. It wasn't just about learning how to walk or do an exercise 'correctly'; it was about the ways my pelvis moved over the top of the thigh bone, and what my back, ribs, shoulders and head had to do with that (for example). It was also about finding the range of possibility through many kinds of movements so I wasn't stuck with the few versions that were associated with pain and weakness. That's the sort of thing lessons explore (pelvic clock for a start!). One of the tricky aspects of pain is that, in seeking to avoid it, we tend to shut down our options more and more – and in the process often limit ourselves to the very pathways that involve it.

These days I run up to a half marathon barefoot, and am currently training for my black belt in Goju Ryu Karate. The training for both those activities has helped strengthen my knees, it's true, but if I hadn't been able to improve or got support from the ground to do any of it, all that strengthening might have served simply to entrench me in painful patterns. And it goes without saying that both those activities are so demanding that I couldn't have even got to the starting line without Feldenkrais. Sometimes in the early days I would experience a difficulty or pain as I upped my mileage or speed, or worked on a new movement in karate. I would get anxious and think about stopping completely. Instead of giving up, though, I would see it as an indication that I needed to improve something. So I would come back to Feldenkrais and delve into lessons that might help and/or go to a senior practitioner for some Functional Integration, until I had improved how I was operating sufficiently for the difficulty to disappear. With the 'how' improved, I could train again, albeit with my attention on training in the better organisation until it was secure. It took considerable dedication but it worked. Very occasionally now when I train hard I strain something – because under pressure I have reverted to an earlier, less useful pattern, or because I just need to find an even better pattern than the ones I have available to cope with this new level of demand – but I have the same attitude: sense what I am doing that is not working so well; use my skill with awareness through movement or seek help from another practitioner to do what I am doing, better. Once I have improved the 'how' I can go back to developing speed, range, amount, power or whatever I want, effectively and safely. Keep going back and forth. Improve. Train. Improve. Train. That way I gain skill instead of simply entrenching unresolved injuries that are likely to deepen and worsen as a result. Win, win. So far, so good.

Interestingly, I didn't go back into acting for long. My life had got to a point where Feldenkrais just seemed a much more interesting and viable option. But had I chosen to, I could have gone back not just 'repaired' but with significantly better awareness and use of myself than before, which is the thing I think is wonderful about Feldenkrais. It is about learning and improving, not just fixing. Sometimes it can help take you beyond an injury into even better functioning than before because of all the attention and learning. And even if it is an injury that is always going to be there in some sense, my observation is that people are not so defined by their injury, are more able to work with and around it, to anticipate a flare-up, and to look after themselves better so the situation doesn't limit them more than necessary (or get even worse). An actor with chronic pain can become unemployable. There is too much money at stake on a shoot or on a tour. Feldenkrais is one of the best tools you can have for staying injury-free, or working with chronic injury if it has got that far.

Awareness Through Movement (ATM)

You can experience ATM work in classes, which are the kind of thing I have put into this book. There are thousands of lessons created by Moshe Feldenkrais, and most experienced teachers also create their own. I have a number of students who come to my classes to find a way out of many kinds of pain or the after-effects of injuries. In these cases, the Method is often very successful, sometimes quickly but sometimes the patterns involved are more deep-seated. Whatever happens, the Method involves learning and improving skill, so it is never wasted time.

Feldenkrais trainer Garet Newell told me about her own experience of injury:

> The one thing the Feldenkrais Method offered that nothing else I had done up till that point seemed to offer was a way to do something for yourself. I felt this could liberate me from that dependence on someone else… by finding a way to direct myself. This is what Awareness Through Movement does. When you are in pain, the person you go to to relieve the pain becomes almost like an addiction in your life. I didn't want that kind of relationship, that kind of dependence.

Classes may not all be suitable for all people with serious difficulty, or who really need another person's touch to address a very specific problem, or to help them stop hurting themselves initially. If your condition prevents you from getting up and down from the floor, then you can still do a considerable number of the lessons in sitting, but many lessons will need to be designed or altered for you: it is important to talk to the teacher first as some are more experienced at doing that than others. Or there is another way you can work…

Functional Integration (FI)

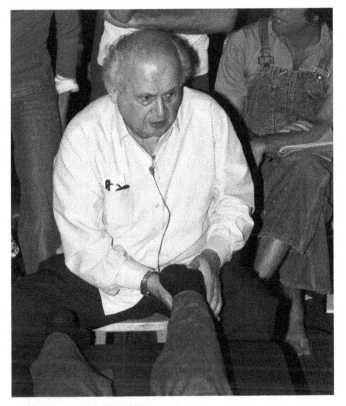

Functional Integration: Moshe Feldenkrais
© International Feldenkrais Federation Archive

Functional Integration is the one-to-one hands-on version of the Method. The aim of FI is still the same as ATM: it is not a different approach, just a different way of experiencing the Method. It is still a way of teaching and enabling rather than 'fixing', but it uses touch and involves a directly relational experience that can be very helpful. FI is also not just for injury: if there is something you wish to improve – be it a skill for art, sport or life – or if you just want a more private, one-to-one experience, then you might be interested to try it out, much as if you wanted to address a specific condition or have too much pain or difficulty to do a class. It is useful for actors working on demands for a particular role too. Some people prefer to do either FI or ATM, and some people do both.

We use a low, wide table and what is sometimes described as a 'listening' touch. It is not massage or cracking or exercising. The practitioner listens to the person with their hands and eyes as well as ears. We feel how the person responds to a small suggestion of movement from our hands or how a small amount of force, like a tiny push through a foot, a shoulder, a rib, a sit bone (for example), can travel through the skeleton. We are trained to 'see' the skeleton and to notice how the different parts of the person join in with the suggested movement and where they don't, where the movement asks for articulation in the skeleton that is not available, where it asks for a connection or relative movement that is not familiar, and also where there are further possibilities. Then with our hands we can bring attention to clarify what is happening in the places that can do the movement well – and even enable you to improve them so your system has a clearer sense of what it is that it is looking for. From there we can go on to invite other places to join in that haven't caught on as easily or have dropped out of the picture. We use some apparently topsy-turvy ways of working, like not stretching muscles that are short from working too hard, but gently bringing the places that the muscles attach a little closer together, so passively shortening them a little more. By this action we take over the work of those muscles and encourage them to give up their work and rediscover their length. We might use rollers and towels and balls to disturb or challenge the status quo in a person's muscle tonus or balance so that their system has to find something different. Just as in ATM, we think about enabling the person to feel the surface beneath them differently, to find support from it through the skeleton and hopefully to have a new experience of themselves in some way.

Functional Integration is a very subtle and enormously skilful art, learnt initially over a four-year training period, but only matured through thousands of hours of experience over many years. We don't dictate with our hands but look for what is already available, going from what the person can do, to gradually introducing a greater variety of possibility. For the practitioner it means having a good understanding of what can be available in a movement and recognising what is and isn't there at any point. It means having a touch that enables the person to recognise something about themselves or go somewhere new without them automatically putting the brakes on before giving it a chance. We have to feel when someone's system feels safe enough and when it is on the edge of feeling pushed too far. We seek to trust the intelligence of the person's system to learn – in the way it has done since the person was a baby – from a variety of experiences, and that a new and better way of operating will emerge as a result, but we have to know how to create the kind of learning experience that will enable that to happen. Sometimes learning can take time and change comes slowly, gradually – two steps forward, one step back, perhaps, and periods of plateauing – but patience is almost always rewarded in the end. Sometimes the change is dramatic and quick. It depends on the person, the skill of the practitioner, the quality of the interaction between them and the particulars of the situation. It is hard to describe the experience. You simply have to try it. All fully qualified Feldenkrais practitioners can offer Functional Integration.

Neuromuscular re-education, functional training and working with an understanding of brain plasticity are now all the rage, but they are the basis for both ATM and FI. I have listed some popular books in the Appendix for further reading. Feldenkrais counted neuroscientist Paul Bach-y-Rita one of the 'grandfathers' of brain plasticity (working on synaesthesia) amongst his friends and colleagues (his wife, Eileen Bach-y-Rita, trained as a Feldenkrais practitioner), and you can listen to his conversation with another well-known neuroscientists of the time, Karl Pribram, on CD. Feldenkrais was already working with how the brain can learn and relearn back in the fifties, and his Method is still one of the most sophisticated available, in my experience. As I write, *New York Times* best-selling science writer Norman Doidge's new book, *The Brain That Heals Itself*, is hitting the shelves with sixty-four pages devoted to Feldenkrais. The recognition is well overdue.

The Pattern of Anxiety

Anxiety can also be a big issue for actors. It can result from the usual stress of producing something special on 'Action!', or in auditions, rehearsals, improvisations, and on first nights, or it can amount to full-on stage fright or camera freeze. Anxiety is also an issue in a wider context, in terms of needing to get work, earn money and deal with the business of trying to build a career. It is also present in every classroom in every drama school where trying to learn from new experiences and diving into the unknown can be a stressful process. The anxiety of getting it right and being good enough or wanted enough can seriously get in the way at every stage in an actor's life. All these things can get in the way of other people's work and lives too, but an actor has to have pretty much all of themselves visibly available and exquisitely able at all times, so anxiety is particularly disruptive.

Having read Part 4a on the physiology of emotion, you will appreciate that much of what I could say about anxiety has been touched on there. The 'fight-or-flight response' or 'stress' are the particular areas of emotional response that everyone knows have a barrage of physiological aspects. These can include targeted blood flow, release of adrenalin and other hormones and transmitters, increased heart and breathing rate, narrowing of vision, suppression of the digestion and immune system, possible release of bowels and bladder, and contraction or inhibition of certain muscle groups, depending on the level of anxiety and fear involved. All these physiological aspects are there to enable us to deal with situations where we need to fight, run or play dead, none of which is very applicable in an acting situation. We do also fluctuate all the time in smaller ways between a higher-alert setting (known as 'sympathetic') of the part of the nervous system, that governs these less (or un)consciously controlled processes ('the autonomic system'); and a more relaxed setting ('parasympathetic'), to enable us to meet the demands of the day or to take advantage of easier moments. An actor can benefit from a certain degree of alertness during performance. But too much and it can easily tip into a fairly full-blown sympathetic state, which can seriously get in the way of moving freely, breathing, speaking, singing, thinking and being easily present and available. Mostly actors wish to find ways to reduce this kind of anxiety and achieve a more helpful balance of the sympathetic and parasympathetic states.

In his book *The Polyvagal Theory*, Stephen Porges presents a more sophisticated version of the sympathetic/parasympathetic axis, centring on the vagal nerve, which is much too complex to go into fully here. Simplified, and as I mentioned in Part 4a, he links our ability to communicate via facial expressions and cues with a calmer state, asserting that a state of high alert 'switches off' our 'social engagement system': very significant for an actor.

In the section on anxiety in his book *The Elusive Obvious*, Feldenkrais points out that the 'flexor' pattern often involved in anxiety or fear (a shortening the muscles of the front and lengthening in the back that produces a curling up) is a protective one. It works not only to shield the vital organs and head from a fall or attack, or can give more force to a subsequent opposite 'extension' pattern (lengthening through the front and upright in the back) which we would need to run away or fight with. The flexor pattern also gives comfort and a feeling of safety that helps to reinstate a sense of well-being, that can in turn calm the anxiety attack.[89] I think many of us know this from the times we are feeling low, when curling up can take us back to some primal place of protectedness that feels safer and so better. This in turn gives us a clue to some of the things that can help in that kind of primal way to calm the sensory aspects of anxiety, and help switch to a more parasympathetic state – to return to a sense of balance, well-being and calm. It is a sense of safety we are looking for at a very fundamental level.

Talking about anxiety, we have to acknowledge that sometimes there is deep underlying trauma, either in the shape of an event or series of events (witnessed or experienced) or in the longer-term (sometimes less dramatic) form of developmental trauma due to the circumstances of a person's childhood. This is an enormous topic and, while we have touched on it in earlier sections – because it is integral to how people shape themselves, how they behave and move – a full discussion of a therapeutic approach for trauma goes beyond the scope of this book.

Support

One of the things that can offer us a feeling of more safety, equilibrium and protection at moments of stress is support: externally that could mean support from anyone on hand who can help in the moment, from family, friends or loved ones, from professionals or from some kind of structure, organisation or from developing a practical solution. Internally the thing that can give us a direct physical sensation of balance and support, and enable some of the holding patterns to let go, is to regain a sense of the skeleton and the ground, since those are the things that literally hold us up. One of the pieces of the anxiety response according to Feldenkrais is inhibition of the anti-gravity muscles. In simpler language, that means the muscles in the legs and around the spine, whose job it is to hold us up against gravity, give up. We have the phrase 'weak at the knees' and the idea that someone can 'crumble' or 'collapse' in the face of too much adversity. This means that everything in Part 2b about sensing the support from the ground, and from the skeleton, and the ability to adjust one's balance and equilibrium, applies here too. A sense of power and potential for power can also give a sense of support and so much in Part 3b can apply too.

There is also something significant in the relational and connective nature of Functional Integration lessons described earlier (a kind of *complicité*, see Part 2a), where the practitioner attends profoundly to the person on the table and gives a sensitive response through touch. Simply being present with them can enable a person to find more of what they need to feel safer and better supported.

Tone

The result of any Feldenkrais lesson, be it Functional Integration or Awareness Through Movement, is usually to reduce unnecessary tension and enable the person to find a more evenly distributed muscular tone throughout, which, being part of a calm state in the autonomic system, can elicit more of the whole state.

Breath

Regulating breath is a widely used technique for working with anxiety, because slowing down the breath and heart rate affects the sympathetic/parasympathetic axis too. The problem is that it can't always be done by willpower in the moment. If you play with the length of the breath or the places that you are breathing into – or if you work with your patterns of breath-holding at times that are not so stressful – you may find that you can make some different patterns more readily available at those stressful times. One aspect to remember is that the in-breath is more activating and the out-breath is more calming, so if you simply increase the length of the out-breath relative to the in-breath you already tilt the axis towards a calmer state. The Feldenkrais Method contains a variety of lessons differentiating the parts you use or could use in breathing, for developing the use of the diaphragm, ribcage and abdomen, clarifying the pathways for breath through the nose or mouth, and working with patterns of inhaling, exhaling, pausing or breath-holding. We have seen an example in Part 5 on breath and voice (*See-Saw Breathing*), but there are many more. Breathing and heart rate are connected through the nervous system, but when you look at the anatomy and notice how the heart sits on top of the diaphragm, it can be no surprise they are linked!

Playfulness

This may be surprising because it's very hard to play when you are anxious, but the opposite is also true: it's very hard to be anxious when you are truly playing. I mentioned the anxiety and stress of learning and how it gets in the way of the student actor – but it could be true in rehearsal and any kind of developmental work. A playful approach to learning is built into the Feldenkrais Method which, if really taken to heart, can take the stress out of many situations an actor finds themselves in.

> I have noticed how much learning is impeded through the anxiety of learning (or is it of being taught?). The anxiety of learning is the fear of appearing stupid or not being able to translate this new information into something that makes sense for you. This is particularly noticeable in the early stages of learning when there is no emergent pattern, or sense of where the movement is going, how it is shaped... which means that you lose your balance; your muscular tonus suddenly becomes unproductively tense and you put yourself in a situation where the movement output is appalling so you are not getting any useful feedback from what you are doing... Feldenkrais gives us an example of how to take a great deal of the anxiety out of learning and put a great deal of the fun and curiosity and self-agency into learning.

> *Dick McCaw,*
> *Senior Lecturer at Royal Holloway, University of London*

What Dick says here is important. There is a duality of opposites that we can get stuck in – right/wrong, yes/no, accepted/not accepted, good/bad – and that can leave us feeling anxious about which side of the duality we will end up on, and feeling shamed if we feel we have ended up in the wrong/no/bad camp. Your teacher, director or colleague can't just tell you that you are right/good all the time, as you wouldn't learn or progress, but what Feldenkrais does effectively is to help you step outside the duality. Feldenkrais isn't about right or wrong, good or bad, yes or no – it's about trying something out and seeing how it goes. Everything is useful as it all contributes to exploring and discovering. If something doesn't work so well for what you want, it's still a step forward because it tells you something. It's closer to play in that sense, because playing can never really be right or wrong (I am talking about creative playing rather than competitive games). Something might be within the rules for the game or not, or be more or less fun, but it isn't wrong in any significant way. If you end up bored or down a blind alley, you just shift the game till it's fun again.

Playfulness also goes with that sense of connectedness to others that can enable a person to feel safer than being stuck on their own with their difficulty. A really palpable example is the way an actor's nerves usually disappear as soon as they feel a connection with the other actors on stage or with the audience. I always remember that first ripple of response or that sense of stillness in the audience that signalled they were with me and that I was not out there on my own gesticulating meaninglessly, or the moment I felt something vital being generated between myself and another actor. I know that some of the pre-show anxiety is about the possibility of this not happening and that you will be left out there on your own to 'die', but as we saw earlier (Part 2a) it is far more likely to happen if you stiffen and become in some way absent. Sometimes you just have to roll with it, acknowledge the connection isn't there yet but stay open and present, without tumbling into the bad/wrong/not accepted side of the duality. The very process of staying open to the possibility of finding a connection can reduce the anxiety level and makes it more likely it will work – whereas stiffening pushes you further away and cuts you off, making you more anxious and ensuring it is less likely that anything will happen. Back in the mid-1980s at the Edinburgh Festival Fringe Club, I saw many an inexperienced comedian get angry because they could not find the connection with the audience quickly enough to get laughs. They would start to shout and stamp about and demand the audience acknowledge them. It never worked. I remember one in particular finally getting a response to his anger. A united chorus of loud, clear, Scottish voices soon finished him off with a simple demand of their own: 'Show us your bum!'

The following is a lesson inspired by American Feldenkrais practitioner, Ralph Strauch, who works in very interesting ways with the physical (somatic) aspects of emotional trauma.[90] *Lesson 13: Patterns of Anxiety* simply aims to give you some idea of how a Feldenkrais lesson affects the way you experience a situation that could make you anxious. I don't know if it will work from reading it rather than doing it with a teacher who can guide you, but maybe, just maybe, it will. And if it does, it will be a very nice way to finish the book.

Lesson 13: Patterns of Anxiety

Before you start, think of something that is making you a little anxious at the moment. Don't pick the hugest, most awful thing, as you don't want to be overwhelmed. Just something that is worrying you or niggling at you. Notice how much it worries you and if there are any sensations associated with that. Any change in breathing, or tension anywhere. Notice when you stop thinking about it what undoes.

Now lie on your back with long legs and notice how you meet the floor. Focus on the difference between the left side and the right side. Does one side lie on the floor differently to the other in your back and pelvis? Does one side feel like it leans more on the ground or has more of it in contact with the ground? How about the difference between the two shoulders too? Is one closer to the floor? Notice how long the two sides feel. Does one side feel longer, bigger or wider than the other? Sometimes it can feel like one leg is longer than the other or there is more space in the waist or ribs.

Pick the side you feel lies more easily on the ground, is less cramped or is some way more comfortable. If you don't have a sense of that just pick either one.

Stay on your back, rest the arm on the chosen side somewhere on the floor above your head. Find a comfortable place where it can rest. If that needs to be more out to the side than straight up that is all right too. If you need to elevate the floor, so your arm can be comfortable in this position, use a cushion or blanket to rest it on.

Keep the leg on that side long, but bend up the opposite knee and plant the foot.

From this starting position, press with the standing foot to roll the pelvis to the other side so one side lifts a little and the other leans more. Go gently and slowly. Notice that you can really just press with the foot and lean the pelvis more on the other side. Take out any unnecessary work or clenching in the abdomen.

Keep pressing and rolling and coming back many times, but begin to direct the push a little higher so you can feel the lower back on the other side come more to the floor. Then the lower ribs on that side, and so on working up the ribs, feeling each time how the turning can travel higher through the spine and a place higher can lean on the floor, until you could even find the shoulder of the arm that is long above your head. Each time you are just pressing to lift one side of the pelvis and rolling the weight into the other side. Notice the leaning more than the lifting. The lifting will take care of itself: it has the support of the ground (as in *Lesson 7: Using the Ground,* p. 125).

Come back to the same movement on the same side and notice if the arm that is long above your head starts to get longer as you press the foot, and roll your weight towards that shoulder. Keep the other one on the floor for now. Does it get a little shorter as you come back?

Try a few times looking up to the hand as it gets longer. Notice how your back has to do something to help your head move so your eyes can look up. Do any other places in that side get longer as your arm does?

Come back to the same position, but this time rest your other arm on your chest or belly. As you press with the foot and roll yourself towards the long arm, let the other shoulder come away from the floor and roll all of you, so that the hand that is across your chest or belly is there to support you on the floor as you come gradually more and more on to your side. Your head may end up on your long arm. Don't force yourself to get there if the long arm is not comfortable. Go as far as you can. Does the long arm want to turn? Is it happy with the palm up or would it like the palm down after a certain point?

If you can get all the way on to your side like this, do so and bring the standing foot a little closer to the long leg (but keep it standing). If you can't, just find your way on to your side and see where you can put your arm and legs that is towards this position. *In this position, wrap the top arm (the one that isn't on the floor) around the top of your head to catch your temple on the other side.*

Lift the head like this with your arm, so the top side of your ribs and waist shortens, and the side on the floor lengthens and leans on the floor more. Notice if an in-breath or out-breath helps the movement more. Again, notice where you can take your support from the floor rather than busy yourself with the effort of lifting.

The same movement, but this time see if it is possible to lift the long leg from the floor a little at the same time as you lift the head. What does your pelvis do to help? Do you feel the waist on the top side shorten even more and somewhere different leaning on the floor? You have the standing leg to help you too.

Roll back on to your back and with both legs long and arms long somewhere at your sides. Feel the difference between the two sides. One might feel easier. Maybe it feels like it has more length or width or connection to the ground.

If the two sides do feel markedly different, in your imagination take yourself into the side that feels in some way clearer, or more comfortable. How does it make you feel as a person to be in this side? Who lives here?

Now take yourself into the other side and feel what it is like to be there. Who is this person? Is it different? In which side do you feel more clarity, ease or sense of well-being?

Go back into the first side and bring up the thing that was worrying you. How worrying does it feel here? Then go into the other side again and notice how much of a problem it feels when you are in that side. Which side might help you find a solution or just feel less at odds?

If you keep swapping from side to side, the differences will probably even up. Or you can just do the same lesson on the other side.

If this works for you it can be quite an eye-opener. Any Feldenkrais lesson can produce greater clarity and ease, and a feeling of well-being can go along with that. All this lesson has done is provide a different experience on the two sides and so helped to show up how that affects the way you experience a situation.

This is how Ralph Strauch put it to me:

> Your experience of a situation doesn't depend just on the situation itself, but on the lens through which you view it. Normally, that lens is smeared and partially obscured by the habitual tensions you carry along subconsciously. The role of the lesson was to clean one side of the lens, so you could experience how obscured your lens ordinarily was. This can act as an incentive to become more aware of your own role in your emotional experience and encourage you to take more positive control over that experience.

Enjoy.

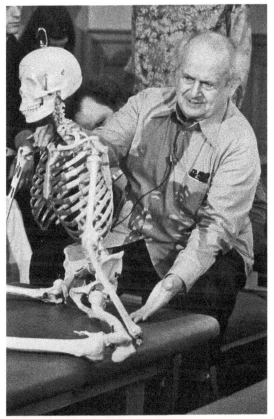

Moshe Feldenkrais in the San Francisco training
from Bob Knighton's collection
© International Feldenkrais Federation Archive

Acknowledgements

Thanks to Shelagh O'Neill and John Wright for their time, support and wise feedback on drafts of this book. Thanks to all in the Feldenkrais community who answered my questions, sent me information, checked whole chapters or little paragraphs, emailed, met, discussed or encouraged me (especially Garet Newell, Maggy Burrowes, Frank Wildman, Dick McCaw, Andrew Dawson, Jeff Haller, Robert Sussuma, Francois Combeau, Ralph Strauch) and, of course, to all my other teachers and colleagues over the years (especially Monika Pagneux and – again – Garet Newell).

A big thank-you also to the theatre practitioners I learnt so much from working with over the years (especially Annie Griffin, Caroline Ward, Theresa Heskins, Sarah Woods and Emma Bernard), and to the drama schools for giving me the opportunity to develop my teaching (especially Oxford School of Drama). *Arigato* to Sensei Kevin Goodman and Sensei Linda Marchant too for a whole new idea of how I could be.

Thanks to all my supportive friends (especially Andrew and Jay), to Andrew Dawson for the use of his studio for the cover photo shoot, and an enormous thank-you to my husband Kevin and daughter Laurel for putting up with me spending all my spare moments on this. Mostly in the kitchen.

Appendix a.
Further Reading and Resources

Hopefully you now wish to rush out and find yourself a Feldenkrais teacher.

You can find up-to-date info on teachers, classes and workshops at the Feldenkrais Guild UK **www.feldenkrais.co.uk**. It also has some free downloads of short lessons and links to many websites.

As an actor, you can learn from any public Awareness Through Movement class, and every Feldenkrais teacher is qualified to do Functional Integration lessons (one-to-one, hands-on sessions, see Part 6) that will address your needs. If you specifically want a teacher with a performance background, you can always check their profile on the Guild website, on their own website, or enquire at your local drama school or university drama course.

Should you wish to train as a professional Feldenkrais practitioner yourself, below are the two professional trainings in the UK (there are also many trainings abroad).

Garet Newell
Feldenkrais International Training Centre
PO Box 36, Hassocks, West Sussex, BN6 8WZ
Phone: 01273 844140
www.feldenkrais-itc.com

Scott Clark
Feldenkrais London
020 8469 0245
www.feldenkraislondon.com/training.html

Resources

You can browse and buy CDs, DVDs and a wide variety of related books at **www.feldenkraisresources.com** and **www.achieveingexcellence.com** (both in the US). Many books are also available in the UK if you order from your local bookstore or look online.

The UK Guild also stock some books and CDs for sale here: **www.feldenkrais.co.uk/further.php**. There is an interesting archive of pictures, videos and documents held by the International Feldenkrais Federation at: **www.feldenkrais-method.org**

A live teacher is important, but you can also find a variety of free downloadable lessons at **www.openatm.org**, and short ones on the UK Guild website at **www.feldenkrais.co.uk/awareness/index.html**

Books

By Moshe Feldenkrais
Higher Judo
Body and Mature Behaviour
Awareness through Movement
The Potent Self
The Elusive Obvious
The Case of Nora
The Master Moves

Also:

Embodied Wisdom: The Collected Papers of Moshe Feldenkrais,
ed. Elizabeth Beringer

On the Feldenkrais Method

The Busy Person's Guide to Easier Movement: 50 Ways to Achieve a Healthy, Happy, Pain-Free and Intelligent Body, Frank Wildman

Change Your Age: Using Your Body and Brain to Feel Younger, Stronger, and More Fit, Frank Wildman

A Guide to Better Movement: The Science and Practice of Moving With More Skill And Less Pain, Todd Hargrove

The Intelligence of Moving Bodies, Carl Ginsberg

Mindful Spontaneity: Lessons in the Feldenkrais Method, Ruthy Alon

Moshe Feldenkrais: A Life in Movement, Mark Reese

Practical Feldenkrais for Dynamic Health, Steven Shafarman

Articles and Research on Feldenkrais in Performance

'The Feldenkrais Method for Actors', Alan Questel in *Movement for Actors*, Nicole Potter (Allworth Press)

'Feldenkrais: Applications for the Actor', Alan Questel in the *Feldenkrais Journal No. 14* **www.harmoniousmovement.com/ Questel_Feldenkrais_for_Actors.pdf**

'Feldenkrais in Theatre and Acting', Andrew Dawson **www.feldenkrais.co.uk/articles/dawson.html**

'Jos Houben: Understanding the Neutral Mask', Anthony Shrubnall in *Jacques Lecoq and the British Theatre*, ed. Franc Chamberlain and Ralph Yarrow (Routledge)

'Feldenkrais Method in performer training: encouraging curiosity and experimentation', Kene Igweonu **create.canterbury.ac.uk/10575/**

Theatre, Dance and Performance Training, Vol. 6, No. 2, A special issue devoted to Feldenkrais, ed. Libby Worth, Jonathan Pitches and Dick McCaw (Routledge), July 2015

'The Resilient Body', Campbell Edinborough in 'Ways of Being a Body' issue of *Body and Performance*, ed. Sandra Reeve (Triarchy Press)

'What Do We Teach?', Campbell Edinborough in *Theatre, Dance and Performance Training* (Routledge), Nov 2013

'Developing Decision-Making Skills in Performance Through Mindfulness in Somatic Training', Campbell Edinborough in *Theatre, Dance and Performance Training* (Routledge), March 2011

'Moving After Auschwitz: The Feldenkrais Method as a Soma-Critique', Thomas Kampe in *Korean Journal of Dance Documentation, Vol. 6*, 2014

'The Art of Making Choices: The Feldenkrais Method as a Choreographic Resource', Thomas Kampe, PhD documentation, London Metropolitan University (unpublished), 2013

'Recreating Histories: Transdisciplinarity and Transcultural Perspectives on Performance Making', Thomas Kampe in *Korean Journal of Dance Documentation, Vol. 67*, 2011

'Weave: The Feldenkrais Method as Choreographic Process', Thomas Kampe in *Perfformio Vol. 1, No. 2*, Spring 2010, pp. 34–52

You can also find a variety of articles on my blog at the bottom of the homepage of my website: **www.feldenkraisworks.co.uk**

A few of the Books, CDs and websites on Feldenkrais for voice and jaw

Maggy Burrowes **www.vocaldynamix.com** and for her many interesting posts and blog

Robert Sussuma **www.robertsussuma.com** including many free videos to watch

Richard Corbeil **www.feldenkraisinseattle.com** and CD: *Vocal Integration*

CD: *The TMJ Program*, Frank Wildman

CD: *TMJ Health*, David Zemach-Bersin and Mark Reese

See one of the online stores above for a bigger list of books and CDs.

Some books and articles on neuroscience, development and anatomy and physiology of movement

Anatomy of Breathing, Blandine Calais-Germain

The Anatomy Coloring Book, Wynn Kapit and Lawrence M Elson

Anatomy of Movement, Blandine Calais-Germain

The Brain That Changes Itself, Norman Doidge

The Brain's Sense of Movement, Alain Berthoz, trans. Giselle Weiss

The Brain's Way of Healing: Remarkable Discoveries and Recoveries from the Frontiers of Neuroplasticity, Norman Doidge

The Challenge of Pain, Melzak and Wall

A Dynamic Systems Approach to the Development of Cognition and Action, Esther Thelen and Linda Smith

'The Improvising Infant' Esther Thelen
infantlab.fiu.edu/articles/Thelen%201996.pdf

The Interpersonal World of the Infant: A View from Psychoanalysis and Developmental Psychology, Daniel Stern

Job's Body: A Handbook for Bodywork, Deane Juhan

Mind Sculpture: Your Brain's Untapped Potential, Ian Robertson

The Physiology of the Joints (three volumes), I. A. Kapandji

The Polyvagal Theory: Neurophysiological Foundatons of Emotions, Attachment, Communication, and Self-Regulation, Stephen Porges

Trauma and the Body: A Sensorimotor Approach to Psychotherapy, Ogden, Minton and Pain

Wider than the Sky: A Revolutionary View of Consciousness, G. M. Edelman

Appendix b. A Postscript for Feldenkrais Teachers

'Are there no technical means by which the actor can achieve the creative mood, so that inspiration may appear oftener than is its wont?' This does not mean that I was going to create inspiration by artificial means. That would be impossible. What I wanted to learn was how to create a favourable condition for the appearance of inspiration by means of the will, that condition in the presence of which inspiration was most likely to descend into the actor's soul...

Stanislavsky[91]

Sound familiar? Didn't Feldenkrais say he didn't *teach* as much as *create the conditions* in which people can learn? That's the job really. The question of how to teach Feldenkrais to actors and acting students does come up often. Does it need to be done differently in some way? Can you just teach a straightforward ATM or does it need to be framed and contextualised, made more specific, or taught slightly differently or as a part of something else?

Personally I think most of these approaches can be valid and it depends on the situation and who you are teaching. An actor can just turn up and do an ATM anywhere in any regular class or workshop, and find the gems within it that relate to them and to what they need if they are open and interested. And they do.

As Garet Newell said to me, the more you frame a lesson, the more something is lost. And she is right – any kind of framework is, by its very nature, limiting. Within that, in the same way that it is possible to teach the same lesson in a public class a number of different ways to bring out different aspects of the lesson, it is possible to teach a lesson in a way that draws attention to aspects that you think will be of particularly of interest to actors.

It is also possible to design a class or a workshop to address something you consider important for actors and teach your ATMs within that framework (in the much same way you might teach a public workshop on a theme) to help elucidate something, and contextualise it with some activities, observations or games that will enable them to apply what they have found. In the same way, if you are working one-to-one with an actor who has come to prepare for a role, you might frame the lesson around what they are exploring and seek to integrate it into skills they can use at the end. It's the same idea that you would apply to anyone who comes for a lesson, class or workshop, just the territory and means of integration may be a little different. For example, I might frame a lesson for a runner with running, or an aspect of running, before and after, so that they notice and integrate whatever they discover. It is also possible to apply Feldenkrais thinking without actually doing a whole ATM in situations where it's necessary to work better and more quickly – I gave some examples in Part 4.

Teaching in drama school is slightly different, though. In that situation you have students who have to be in your class because it is part of the course. They have not chosen to be there, may know nothing about Feldenkrais, and may start without much of an interest in movement or understanding of why it is important for actors. Their purpose in coming to the school is to learn to be an actor and make a good career in the business rather than personal development (although that is an inevitable part of any learning process), but they cannot leave your class if they don't find it useful and cannot see its relevance. The onus may be on them to learn, but it is also on you as a teacher to offer them as many ways in to the Method as possible, and to respond to their level of need for a framework which will make it accessible and useable: to create an environment in which they can learn.

What that environment is will differ. Third years are different to first years, who are different again to post-grads or foundation-course students; music-theatre students are different to acting students; one school is different to another; one group of first years is different to another. How Feldenkrais sits within the school may be different, how integrated it is into the different departments, and how the rest of the staff respond to it and accommodate it will vary. Your position within the school and with those students may make a difference too. All of that has to be taken into account in what you do and may make it easier or harder.

Your students may be very 'with' you and able to get what they need just from a straightforward series of ATMs. On the other hand, you may find you want to frame what they are doing more or use more games to capture their imaginations or clarify what is useful about the changes that come about in a lesson. You may want to include pair and observational work to give them more ownership of the lessons. Group or pair work can give them the opportunity to see or feel the changes in each other and have their own changes witnessed: it may be that others can see or feel changes in them that they cannot feel in themselves, or they may see or feel changes in others that make them look for those kinds of possibilities in themselves. They may hear difference in their voice before they notice anything else.

You may want to start with bigger lessons first, in which they can learn to do something like getting up and down from the floor in different ways to challenge them. Discovering that they can learn to do something big like that with considerably more ease, very quickly, will enable them to move on to smaller, more detailed work that takes greater patience and finer levels of sensitivity. You might find you have students with a lot of difficulties on the floor and so you have to stay away from anything challenging for some time, tailoring the work very carefully. You may have a group that is ready to dive right in to highly nuanced work and relish it, or you may want to create situations where they are likely to have very strong experiences to bring the work alive (like the sand boxes). You might want to involve them in an external observational project that relates to a theme you are exploring, so that they are applying what they are discovering in themselves to what they can see in a stranger's walk, gestures, presence or behaviour – and notice what story they get from that or what parts of it they can in turn try out for themselves. You may be able to relate the lessons to what they need for a show or a project/course they are doing with another teacher, in order to create a context that helps them see how they can use it.

I have listed just a few possibilities. Most teachers who go to work in drama schools have a performance background so most will have a wealth of ideas of their own to draw on to make it work in their own way. In good Feldenkrais tradition it may take a bit of trial and error. A few 'approximations'. Confidence and experience helps and also knowing that, however well you teach, you can't win 'em all.

I hope the book offers some food for thought and a few ideas to build on.

Endnotes

1. It is possible that Volume 2 of Feldenkrais's biography will elucidate this when it comes out.

2. The interview with Moshe Feldenkrais by Dennis Levi in *Embodied Wisdom*, ed. Elizabeth Beringer, pp. 126–60, entitled 'The extraordinary story of how Moshe Feldenkrais came to study judo' is a wonderful read.

3. *The Brain's Way of Healing*, Norman Doidge, pp. 160–61.

4. *Ibid.*, p. 164.

5. For example, *Higher Judo (Groundwork)* (in print); *ABC of Judo* and *Judo the Art of Defense and Attack* (out of print).

6. The details of this are wonderful – e.g. it was Ian Fleming (creator of James Bond) who organised the evacuation.

7. *Hadaka-Jime: The Core Technique for Practical Unarmed Combat* (in print).

8. For a brief history of Peter Brook's working life, see *Actor Training*, Alison Hodge, pp. 185–7, article by Lorna Marshall and David Williams.

9. For more detail about Feldenkrais's life, see *Moshe Feldenkrais: A Life in Movement*, Mark Reese; *The Brain's Way of Healing*, Norman Doidge, Chapter 5; *Making Connections, Hasidic Roots in the Teachings of Moshe Feldenkrais*, David Kaetz.

10. *The Conference of the Birds*, John Heilpern, p. 99.

11. *Ibid.*, p. 146.

12. *Actor Training*, Alison Hodge, p. 219, article by Simon Murray.

13. *Inside/Outside*, Robert Golden Pictures, available to stream on the internet or buy.

14. *Jacques Lecoq*, quoted by Simon Murray.

15. 'A New Look at Infancy' in *The Intelligence of Moving Bodies*, Carl Ginsberg; *The Elusive Obvious*, Moshe Feldenkrais, pp. 29–37; *A Dynamic Systems Approach to the Development of Cognition and Action*, Esther Thelen and Linda Smith.

16. *Mind Sculpture*, Ian Robertson, pp. 26–34, and *passim*; *Wider than the Sky*, GM Edelman, p. 29.

17. 'The Improvising Infant', Esther Thelen http://infantlab.fiu.edu/articles/ Thelen%201996.pdf.

18. *A Basis for Sensorimotor Development – Normal and Abnormal*, MR Fiorentino, p. 42.

19. *Trauma and the Body*, Pat Ogden et al, p. 19, incl: 'Todd (1959) taught that function precedes structure: the same movement over and over again moulds the body, e.g. when the muscular contractions that prime defensive movements are repeated many times, these contractions turn into physical patterns that affect the body's structure, which in turn affects further functions... and even sustains corresponding emotions and cognitions.'

20. *The Potent Self*, Moshe Feldenkrais, pp. 23–9.

21. *The Interpersonal World of the Infant*, Daniel Stern, pp. 38–68.

22. *Mind Sculpture*, Ian Robertson, pp. 26–34, and *passim*.

23. Neuroscientist Jonathon Cole on proprioception and the loss of it: vimeo.com/30740202; Ian Waterman: vimeo.com/30663942.

24. vimeo.com/20119968, 46 minutes in.

25. *Job's Body*, Deane Juhan, pp. 186–190; *Trauma and the Body*, Pat Ogden et al, p. 19.

26. *A Guide to Better Movement*, Todd Hargrove, p. 286, re: role of attention in neuroplasticity quotes: (note 41) 'Attention seems to work at the level of the synapse, strengthening certain connections and inhibiting others.' Farran Briggs, George R Mangun, W Martin Usrey (2013), (note 42) 'Attention amplifies neural activity associated with the sensory input to which attention is directed.' Kerr and Shaw (2008); 'Tactile Acuity in Experienced Tai Chi Practitioners: Evidence for Use Dependent Plasticity as an Effect of Sensory-Attentional Training' in *Experimental Brain Research*, *Vol. 188, No. 2*, June 2008, pp. 317–22 http://www.ncbi.nlm.nih.gov/pmc/articles/PMC2795804.

27. *The Intelligence of Moving Bodies*, Carl Ginsberg, p. 286 for an explanation of the self-image. CG also quotes 'What We Are Naming',

M. Sheets Johnstone and 'Dynamic Models of Body Schematic Processes', Shaun Gallagher, p. 234 in *Body Image and Body Schema: Interdisciplinary Perspectives on the Body*, ed. Helena De Preester & Veroniek Knockae.

28. *A Guide to Better Movement*, Todd Hargrove, p. 285 (note 33) re: famous study by Allard, Clark, Jenkins, Merzenich (1991): 'Reorganisation of somatosensory area 3b representations in adult owl monkeys after digital syndacactyl', *AJP JN Physiol Vol. 66, No. 3*, September 1991 http://jn.physiology.org/content/66/3/1048.abstract.

29. Interview about Feldenkrais with Dr Michael Merzenich, Professor Emeritus at the University of San Francisco, co-founder and Chief Scientific Officer at Posit Science, https://youtu.be/rupZ-wlRdA0.

30. *Ibid.*

31. *Awareness Through Movement*, Moshe Feldenkrais, p. 10.

32. *The Moving Body*, Jacques Lecoq, pp. 39–40.

33. *A Guide to Better Movement*, Todd Hargrove, p. 85.

34. *On Acting*, Sanford Meisner, p. 24.

35. 'Moshe Feldenkrais discusses Awareness and Consciousness with Aharon Katzir' in *Embodied Wisdom*, ed. Elizabeth Beringer, pp. 175–6.

36. *On Acting*, Sanford Meisner, p. 36.

37. Well worth bringing in here too is Campbell Edinborough's valuable article 'Developing decision-making skills for performance through the practice of mindfulness in somatic training' in *Theatre, Dance and Performance Training, Vol. 2, Issue 1*, p. 18, in which he compares the awareness that both an actor or martial artist needs Langer's notion of 'mindfulness'. Campbell draws his experience from his Aikido practice; I draw mine from my practice of Goju Ryu Karate-do; Feldenkrais drew his from his mastery of Judo.

38. Bruce Lee 'lost interview', 12 minutes 20 seconds in: archive.org/details/BruceLeeTheLostInterview.

39. *On Acting*, Sanford Meisner, p. 42: 'Acting isn't talking, acting is feeding off the other fellow'.

40. Some other relevant precepts in the Bubishi are:
Distance and posture will dictate the outcome of the meeting.
The eyes do not miss even the slightest change.
The ears listen well in all directions, *or* (a different translation) expect the unexpected.

41. *Theatre, Dance and Performance Training*, George Mann, Nov 2013: an edited transcript from an interview by Dick McCaw.

42. *On Acting*, Sanford Meisner, p. 8.

43. Stanislavsky: choose a transitive verb to describe as accurately as possible what you want to do to the other actor with that line or phrase.

44. *Inside/Outside*, Robert Golden Pictures.

45. *The Potent Self*, Moshe Feldenkrais, p. 237.

46. *Ibid.*, pp. 53–61 and 109–26, and *The Elusive Obvious*, Moshe Feldenkrais, pp. 39–54.

47. Video footage of Moshe Feldenkrais lecture at Cern. Currently unavailable.

48. *Anna Karenina*, first sentence in Chapter 1, as quoted in *A Guide to Better Movement*, Todd Hargrove, p. 12.

49. Introduction to *Higher Judo, passim*, and *The Elusive Obvious Moshe Feldenkrais*, p. 43: 'Human Posture, in spite of the implications of the static "posting", is a dynamic equilibrium. A posture is good if it can regain equilibrium after a large disturbance.' Recently well presented in practice by Shihan Moti Nativ (Bujinkan Ninjitsu), who has explored the martial roots of Feldenkrais in a series of workshops available on DVD called *The Warrior's Awareness*.

50. In his advanced workshop *Finding the Internal Roots of Strength*.

51. www.physio-pedia.com/Centre_of_Gravity.

52. From the Bubishi, quoted in Part 2a.

53. See Part 1 on learning, p. 29.

54. A member of El Teatro Campesino in discussion with Moshe Feldenkrais at end of the workshop with Peter Brook's actors, July 1973, in San Juan Bautista. CD: *Questions and Answers, Feldenkrais with Peter Brook and El Teatro Campesino*.

55. *Theatre of Movement and Gesture*, Jacques Lecoq, pp. 89–91.

56. Moshe Feldenkrais in an interview with Richard and Helen Schechter entitled 'Image, Movement and Actor: Restoration of Potentiality', *Embodied Wisdom*, ed. Elizabeth Beringer, p. 103.

57. *Inside/Outside*, Robert Golden Pictures.

58. For an article on WF in relation to Feldenkrais: www.semiophysics.com/SemioPhysics_Articles_mental_10.html.

59. *Embodied Wisdom*, ed. Elizabeth Beringer, p. 101; and also see www.cns.nyu.edu/~msl/courses/0044/handouts/Weber.pdf.

60. *The Application of WF in Feldenkrais Method*, https://youtu.be/nxTW4-hewGU.

61. CD: *Questions and Answers, Feldenkrais with Peter Brook and El Teatro Campesino.*

62. *Feldenkrais for Artists in NYC*, blog post on Feldenkrais and clowning www.feldenkraisarts.com/feldenkrais-and-clowning.

63. *Inside/Outside*, Robert Golden Pictures.

64. *Theatre of Movement and Gesture*, Jacques Lecoq, p. 98.

65. *Actor Training*, ed. Alison Hodge, chapter on Jacques Copeau by Jon Rudin, p. 57.

66. *The Moving Body*, Jacques Lecoq, p. 41.

67. *Embodied Wisdom*, ed. Elizabeth Beringer, interview with Richard and Helen Schechner, p. 108.

68. physicsclassroom.com/class/newtlaws/Lesson-3/Newton-s-Second-Law.

69. www.sportsrehabexpert.com/public/195.cfm, scroll down to the end of the written article.

70. *Embodied Wisdom*, ed. Elizabeth Beringer, interview with Richard and Helen Schechner, p. 103.

71. *Inside/Outside*, Robert Golden Pictures.

72. *Embodied Wisdom*, ed. Elizabeth Beringer, interview with Dennis Levi on judo, pp. 152–3.

73. All Ute Hagen references from *A Challenge for the Actor*, especially Chapter 7: 'The Psychological Senses', pp. 83–99.

74. *Trauma and the Body*, Pat Ogden et al, p. 11.

75. *Embodied Wisdom*, ed. Elizabeth Beringer, p. 94.

76. *Ibid.*, p. 95.

77. *An Actor Prepares*, Konstantin Stanislavsky, p. 84.

78. *To the Actor*, Michael Chekhov, p. 2.

79. *On Acting*, Sanford Meisner, p. 69.

80. *The Brain's Way of Healing*, Norman Doidge, p. 326.

81. *The Polyvagal Theory*, Stephen Porges.

82. Lakoff and Johnson, pp. 43–4, quoted in *Trauma and the Body*, Pat Ogden et al, pp. 9–10.

83. It is a little more complicated than this, in fact, as the pelvis also gyrates, which involves more complex directions, but I am keeping it simple for this book.

84. www.feldenkraisarts.com, blog post on Feldenkrais and clowning.

85. http://www.nytimes.com/2008/02/17/magazine/17play.html.

86. *A Life in Movement*, Mark Reese, p. 30.

87. Maggy Burrowes, www.vocaldynamix.com/blog.
Robert Sussuma, www.robertsussuma.com including many free videos to watch.
Richard Corbeil, www.feldenkraisinseattle.com, and *Vocal Integration* CD.

88. *Finding the Roots of Internal Strength*, Jeff Haller, advanced training for practitioners.

89. This is so central to the Feldenkrais Method that there are also significant chapters on anxiety in his other books: *Body and Mature Behaviour* and *The Potent Self*.

90. See more about Ralph Strauch at his website www.somatic.com, including blogs and articles.

91. *My Life in Art*, Konstantin Stanislavsky, pp. 461–2.

Index of Games and Lessons

Games

Lessons